CW01666764

The Emotional Yoga Experience: Use Your Body To Heal Your Mind

by

Daralyse Lyons

Published by Martin Brown Publishers, LLC

1138 South Webster Street
Kokomo, Indiana 46902
www.mbpubs.com

ISBN: 978-1-937070-52-6

Table of Contents

Acknowledgements

I would like to acknowledge all of the people whose support and encouragement made this book possible.

Thank you to Jay Wurts who helped me find my authorial voice. You were alternately a therapist, a cheerleader, and a truth-teller. If not for your professionalism and your understanding of the industry, my book would still be a dream and would never have become a reality. Thank you for your investment in EYE and your valuable contributions both on and off the page.

Dexter Wetmore, I can't even begin to express how grateful I am for all of your diligence and professionalism. Your photographs make *The Emotional Yoga Experience* the rich, visual text that it is.

Thank you to Twisters Yoga Studio for providing space to take photographs and to studio owners Trisha and Toby Fleming for all of the generosity and support that you offer the yoga community.

I am grateful to the owners of Indigo Schuy. Thank you for donating the incredibly flattering clothing for *The Emotional Yoga Experience* photo shoot. Your outfit enabled me to look more put-together than usual. I recommend that anyone who ever has occasion to be in Chestnut Hill, Pennsylvania, visit this quaint yoga-wear boutique.

Thank you to my marketing consultant, Josh Minlind, who believed in EYE even before there was something to believe in. Special thanks to Robert and Sharene Brown of Martin Brown Publishers, LLC. It is only due to your tireless, thoughtful work that this book morphed from a dream into a reality.

I am especially grateful to my friends and family who saw me through countless drafts and revisions and who offered encouragement and insight throughout the publishing process. Your support, love, and dedication helped tremendously.

To the yoga community at large, my yoga teachers, and those who believe in the innate wisdom of the body, thank you for teaching me the true path to healing. I hope that I can illuminate that path for others.

To Gary Craig, the founder of EFT, your genius astounds me and, after getting to know you, I am touched not only by your wisdom but by your modesty. Your teachings are the basis for the positive energy shifts that enable me to continually heal myself, and others, with EYE.

I am especially grateful to my clients who provided the inspiration for this book and whose stories I trust will allow readers to find healing within these pages.

Last, but not least, thank you to you, the reader. It is for you that this book was written. Every time I felt discouraged or overwhelmed or bumped up against a closed door, I thought of you and knew that the next story of healing that I want to tell is yours. Please read these pages, apply them to your life, and let my love for you and gratitude towards you wash over you. You deserve to live the fullest life possible. Thank you for giving my life and my work purpose.

Namaste.
(*The light in me honors the light in you.*)

This book is dedicated to my mother. She loved me long before I ever learned to love myself.

Disclaimer

The techniques and suggestions presented in this book are not a substitute for professional medical or mental health advice. Not all exercise is suitable for everyone; therefore, you should always consult with a licensed health-care provider before beginning any new exercise regimen or any type of therapy program.

• If you are new to yoga, it is recommended that you work with a professional yoga instructor prior to trying any of the poses outlined in this book.

• The American Yoga Association does not recommend yoga for pregnant or nursing women or for children under 16 years of age.

• It is suggested that menstruating women refrain from performing inverted poses, back bends or vigorous standing poses.

• Always consult with a medical practitioner, especially if you have a special health consideration of any kind, before performing any exercise or starting a new health program of any kind.

• If you are elderly or have any chronic or recurring conditions such as high blood pressure, neck or back pain, arthritis, heart disease, etc., it is especially important that you seek your physician's advice before practicing any form of yoga.

• The author and/or publisher assume(s) no responsibility for injuries suffered while attempting or practicing the techniques shown in this book.

Author's Note

Because the work I do is highly confidential, professional ethics require that I alter names and details in such a way as to make it impossible to discern the identity of any one of my clients. As such, I've taken creative license with names, ages, demographics, and other non-essential information so as to mask the identities and preserve the privacy of those who come to me for help. However, the essentials are all unchanged. The emotions, the poses, and the level of relief as well as many of the EYE and EFT set-up phrases contained within these pages remain fundamentally unaltered.

As you utilize the healing methodologies presented here, please remember this book is not meant as a sole resource. Physical, mental, and emotional wellness require a holistic approach. I urge you to look to this text as a source of self-help and not as a substitute for qualified allopathic and alternative treatments. You are responsible for your own physical, mental, and emotional health. I hope my experiences and those of my clients will aid you in your quest for a whole and happy life. Use this book and the practices herein to emerge from the pain of your past as you learn to embrace the joy of the present and the promise of a better, unencumbered future.

Introduction

You are no doubt wondering how the Emotional Yoga Experience (EYE) can help you to positively transform your life. If you are suffering from persistent physical or emotional issues such as anxiety, depression, post-traumatic stress disorder, addiction, stress, chronic pain or emotional eating issues, EYE offers an extremely effective, body-based approach to diagnosing and treating what ails you. If you feel hopeless and stuck, if you don't know where to turn to get help, or if you feel incapable of making the changes you want to make in your life, The Emotional Yoga Experience has the potential to liberate you from your limiting emotional and behavioral patterns. Even if your issues are more subtle and less specific, even if you can't quite identify or verbalize your problems, EYE has the potential to help you feel better.

Most of us have experienced times when we knew, rationally, that we needed to change and yet were incapable of self-transformation. If you're anything like I once was, or like many of my clients were, you have experimented with talk-therapy, psychiatry, positive affirmations, guided meditation, hypnosis, or a litany of other approaches to self-healing that are aimed at changing your mind in order to change your feelings. Have these conventional and alternative treatments been ineffective for you? They certainly didn't work for me! In fact, no matter how much I wanted to think my way to wellness, I was incapable of changing myself through willpower, positive thinking, or behavior modification. The reason these approaches never worked for me, and might have been ineffective for you, is that our minds cannot and will not cure our emotional problems.

If your emotional issues cause you to feel like you are "losing your mind," I say "Good. You've come to the right place. Your mind is part of the problem."

It is not your fault that your attempts to get well through brain power and mental gymnastics haven't worked. Trying to think your way out of emotional pain is like trying to think your way out of physical pain. Imagine how ludicrous it would be to tell a woman going through intense pain during childbirth to "think away the pain." She would probably respond with a few choice words for you. Emotional anguish is just like those excruciating, all-consuming labor pains.

You can't think away your agony. Only a physical experience can move you past your hurts. Negative emotions live in your body and it requires a rearrangement of your body's physical energy to release negative feelings and replace them with positive ones. The mind is limited in what it can do. With the Emotional Yoga Experience, prepare to step out of your mind and into your body, to reset your physical energy and to emerge emotionally healthy and whole.

The Emotional Yoga Experience offers a nonverbal approach to healing that circumvents the mind and heals unhealthy emotions physically and energetically rather than cognitively. EYE is unlike any other approach to wellness because it both diagnoses and treats emotional issues physically. You won't have to spend hours on a therapist's couch or thousands of dollars to get well. All you will need is a yoga mat and this book, which includes step-by-step techniques that enable you to nonverbally diagnose and heal your unwanted emotions. Simple, effective, prescriptive, and rapid, EYE's instructional exercises provide a way out of your pain.

How does EYE help you, wanting desperately to get out of your own painful behavioral and emotional patterns, to heal once and for all? How can you rid yourself of your own internal blockages and heal fully and effortlessly? In this book, you will read about others who, like yourself, have felt hopeless and have tried everything. Following their examples, you will discover how to feel and release your emotions physically. Yoga offers a doorway into the dark room of your emotions and EFT flips on the light switch, illuminating the space that had once been obscured by blackness.

Yoga alone is unlikely to bring about emotional healing. It offers physical and emotional awareness, but it leaves the body's energy system unchanged. It can provide relief, but does not repair the damage (like taking an aspirin for a broken bone). Similarly, because it relies on cognitive self-assessment, EFT is limited as a diagnostic tool. The Emotional Yoga Experience transcends both yoga and EFT because it identifies and releases trapped negative emotions. Using EYE, we set traditional talk-therapy aside and address the body's energy system directly. We talk to the body in a way that it can understand and interpret – using the language of motion.

If we trust our bodies over our minds, you may be wondering about finding rational explanations for our behaviors. Where does reason fit in?

From my own self-healing experiences and from working with clients, I have discovered that it is possible to fully heal without knowing, precisely, where or why an energy impasse has occurred. In fact, the more desperate and blocked you feel, and the greater your emotional release experience, the less you might care where your suffering originated. You'll likely just want move forward differently. Besides, much of the behavior that you are looking to change is probably pretty irrational anyway, right? I mean how, exactly, is a pint of ice cream supposed to help heal your wounded pride when you are stood up for a date? It can't. Yet, that won't keep you from reaching for ice cream after a heartbreak. The intellect often fails to explain our pain or our behaviors because our actions aren't driven by reason but spring from our bodies' primal urges and energetic blockages. Balance your energy, and your life will improve whether or not you ever understand the origins of your issues.

As a practitioner, I have seen clients with depression, anxiety, phobias, addictions and a host of other issues freed from their emotional pain by the physical acts involved during their Emotional Yoga Experiences. Many of them never discovered the source of their emotional injuries, yet the pain generated by those wounds evaporated with EYE. Our rationalizations satisfy the expectations of talk-therapists and offer us temporary relief, but the results are fleeting and often deceptive.

The body never lies. It can't. So, until we permanently change our bodies' energy, our symptoms – physical, emotional, and psychic pain – inevitably come back.

Still skeptical about the technique? Don't think EYE can work for you? Think you are different and nothing else has worked so why will this? Great! No problem. Your thoughts don't have any impact on whether or not this approach will work for you. It doesn't matter what you think about EYE. Whether or not you believe that these techniques will work on your emotional issues is immaterial because EYE operates at the level of the body. The techniques will work for you even if you don't believe that anything can help you to heal. How do I know this? Because I have seen it hundreds of times and experienced it myself, again and again.

EYE works. Believe it. Or, don't believe it. Just try it. The results speak for themselves.

The Birth of the Emotional Yoga Experience

I am a walking testimonial for EYE. After having been trapped in a raging eating disorder for twelve years, I cured myself of bulimia in about fifteen minutes by combining yoga and the Emotional Freedom Technique (EFT) in what I would later come to call the Emotional Yoga Experience.

As a depressed, suicidal bulimic, I had worked with therapists, psychiatrists, and other treatment professionals to try to understand and cure my disease using brain power and behavior modification. Twelve years of conjecture, guesswork, and psychoanalysis and the result was an impressive list of plausible, rational explanations for my totally irrational, implausible, and self-destructive behavior. Cognitive awareness got me nowhere. My mind was powerless over my body. For me, true healing meant "going out of my mind" and re-entering my body.

When I first started practicing yoga, I sat in silence. With nobody listening and no place to go, my emotions floated to the surface like dead goldfish in a bowl. Through yoga, I became aware of the stored body-pain that had accumulated over years of emotional trauma and had found voice in a rampant eating disorder. I sat cross-legged on the mat and wept copiously, feeling the tears of a lifetime roll down my cheeks. I later discovered that this is not an unusual reaction for a novice yogi encountering her own, quiet soul for the first time.

Later, I stumbled onto the Emotional Freedom Technique (EFT). EFT works by displacing the body's negative energy the way light displaces darkness at the flip of a switch. When we experience negative emotions, our energy shuts down. EFT restores the flow of positive, useful energy by using various points on the body like light switches. Generally, EFT practitioners help their clients to discover specific blockages through talk-therapy followed by "flipping the switch" with EFT's "tapping" technique (a kind of non-invasive emotional acupressure). My early experiences with EFT involved the use of talk-therapy followed by this "tapping." Despite feeling like EFT, used on its own (without yoga), helped take the edge off of some of my emotions, I remained stuck in my self-destructive behaviors. Something was still missing. I was still locked in my self-perpetuated pattern of victimization and abuse, binging and purging. Why?

The main problem was that conventional EFT uses talk-therapy to uncover emotional issues, and thereby creates the illusion that we can see ourselves clearly and rationally understand the irrational. That is, we put our brains in charge of a process that properly belongs to our bodies. The body holds memories that are pre-verbal. It doesn't lie. It can't, because deception – even self-deception – is a cognitive act. EFT works because it enlists the body as an ally in the effort to unblock our stuck energy. However, it still leaves the brain in charge of diagnosis, and cognition can only go so far.

When I finally tuned into (with yoga) and released (with EFT) the energy that had been bottled up within me for so long, spontaneous healing happened. I asked my body the question that I had asked my mind over and over for years: What emotion drives your bulimia? Yoga turned a sudden spotlight on the answer that had always eluded me – fear. Through Tree Pose, I connected with the fear that my body had been holding onto, subconsciously, since childhood. As a child, I had suffered a series of grand mal seizures. Nothing gets your attention faster than being absolutely out of control of your body. Worst of all, it put me in a perpetual state of panic: I feared that I was going to die.

As I stood in Tree Pose, wobbly, off-balance and terrified, the memories of my violent epileptic episodes came flooding back. I relived that same childhood fear. Realization dawned on me that whenever I binged and purged it was to regain the feeling of control that I'd lost as a child. I couldn't, and wouldn't, stop this self-destructive behavior because bulimia worked. It helped me, momentarily, feel safe. Every time I tortured myself, I felt a false sense of empowerment. During all of my years of psychotherapy, I had never before identified this early childhood reaction to a premature sense of my own mortality as the cause of my bulimia. Why would I? There were so many other events and experiences that therapists told me were the classic causes of my behavior. Who was I to question them? Moreover, I had blocked out the memory of these seizures, recalling the fact of their existence but not their traumatic impact on me.

Yoga revealed to me a level of subliminal awareness that exists in everyone, all the time, but too often goes unnoticed. I then used EFT to "tap out" the fears I had experienced in childhood that continued to drive my bulimia. These emotions resided deep within my body (outside of the scope of my mind). EFT allowed me to release the feelings that had enslaved me for years. I needed a physical experience to change me on an emotional level. And that is just what happened in that moment, on my mat. The result was miraculous!

As it turned out, this experience happened immediately following a session of binging and purging. My apartment was full of binge food, since I had planned a day of frenzied bulimia. However, the moment yoga put a finger on my fear and EFT gave it a path to leave my body, an internal shift took place. I became incapable of binging and purging – literally. I remained in my apartment, surrounded by my bulimic buffet, but could not bring myself to touch it. The desire to binge and purge was gone and did not return. Aside from great relief, I began to sense that I had experienced something deeply profound and lasting.

Since that day, I have developed and refined the Emotional Yoga Experience – a proven, transformational approach to wellness that engages the body and transforms lives. I began working with others who, like myself, had found healing elusive. Contrary to everything that I had thought and been taught, I realized that a talking "cure" offered little more than a bandage for emotional wounds. On the other hand, by connecting to the emotions contained within our bodies and recalibrating our physical energy, we can cure our emotional injuries and live our lives to the fullest.

Explore: Use Yoga to Excavate Your Innermost Feelings

I used to set foot on a yoga mat and cry. Those first few minutes of class, seated in a cross-legged position, focusing on my breath and establishing an intention were torture. Suddenly, tears would stream down my face. I wondered if someone would notice and kick me out of class. When would the pain be over? Excruciating corporal punishment – that's what gentle yoga felt like to me. The stillness was agonizing. Slowly integrating my mind and my body made me alternately sad and angry.

Likewise, my clients often experience deep internal shifts on the mat. Their emotional wounds open as they weep within the space and safety of silence. As they connect with their feelings, they are often surprised by the stories that their bodies tell.

Holly, Lisa, and Tim

Holly's Yoga Experience:

Thirty-two years old, with strikingly beautiful raven hair, Holly had been diagnosed with borderline personality disorder. She came to see me because neither medication nor talk-therapy had proven effective for her.

"I'm a borderline," she told me, looping a large red scrunchie around her long mane. "I'm not really sure what else to say. That's a lot to deal with."

In Downward Dog, Holly began to scream – an intense, agonized wail that seemed to emanate from somewhere deep within her. She vividly described slashing her wrists during her most recent suicide attempt (there had been three). The blood-red scrunchie dangled mockingly as she saw the razor clearly in her mind's eye. She pressed her hands into the mat, closed her eyes, and together we transported her back into the pain of her past. My fingers moving along her spine gently knocked on the door to her emotions. Her mind had told her for so long that her past suicide attempts no longer bothered her, but her body told her differently. After the screams subsided, her tears came. Her body shook; her voice trembled. As her body divulged the true source of her pain, Holly kept her eyes closed tight.

Explore Your Emotions

Downward Dog

Begin on hands and knees on your yoga mat with your knees directly underneath your hips and your hands slightly in front of your shoulders. Curl your toes under, pressing your hands firmly on the mat. Straighten your arms and legs, lengthening your tailbone, and broaden your back. Your body should now form an upside down V-shape. Separate each vertebrae as if it were a single pearl along the longer spinal strand. Imagine that stored sadness sits at the base of your spine and imagine this sadness flowing outward from your tailbone down your arms, out through your hands, down your legs and out your heels. Tune into your feelings of sadness as each exhalation brings you deeper into the sensation. Fully focus on your feelings. Don't avoid them. Stay with each emotion.

When I began doing yoga, it felt disorienting. Yoga involved stepping out of my mind and into my body, as if I were veering away from self-deception, and into the truth of my own lived experience. My body was screaming to tell me something. Anytime that I stood still and breathed deeply, I cried. I was in mental, physical and emotional pain. So why did I keep doing yoga?

Paradoxically, I noticed that between classes it was helping me. I hated stepping "out of my mind" and into my body; however, the more I did it, the quieter my obsessive thoughts became, and the more integrated I felt: less stressed and more centered. Sometimes, yoga even reduced my bulimic behavior.

Lisa's Yoga Experience:

Likewise, Lisa needed to escape her mind and enter her body. Like I had once been, she was initially uncomfortable with this transition from the intellectual to the experiential. As a highly competent, intelligent woman, Lisa mentally discounted her childhood experiences because she thought she had outgrown them.

"This is ridiculous! I didn't come here to crouch in Child's Pose and make myself feel small. I came here to move past my emotional insecurities. I've done the 'inner-child' work, damn it! This is a waste of time. In ten seconds, I plan to call it quits. How long have I been holding this stupid Child's Pose anyway? I am not a child!"

Her vehemence failed to mask her vulnerability.

Whispering softly into her ear, I told her to let go. "It's okay to be a child."

With that permission, Lisa unclenched. Tears rose to the surface. I let her feel what she needed to feel. She remained in Child's Pose for a long time, her bowed head and curved back obscuring everything but her red hair and gray-green sweater. I heard the whimper of a child's voice.

"Mommy," she murmured over and over until, suddenly, she came back to the present moment to find that her mat was wet with her tears.

She looked up at me. A few freckles dotted her nose. Her expression was nakedly innocent, made so by her baby-blue eyes and the shyest shade of a smile.

"I wonder who it was who cried so hard – me or that 'inner-child' I thought had grown up a long time ago," the upturn of her lips was tentative, her smile uncertain.

I reassured her that, although she was no longer a child, her body felt stuck.

She then began to talk about how, as a young girl, her voice never mattered. Lisa's mother had gotten pregnant with her to save her marriage. It didn't work and her father left anyway, leaving Lisa's single mother resentful. On the mat, in Child's Pose, Lisa connected with her feeling of invisibility – a feeling that her body had held onto since her childhood.

"If you had a voice and could say whatever you always wanted to say, but your mother was never willing to hear, what would you tell her?" I questioned.

Without hesitation, her answer came: "I need you to love me."

Explore Your Emotions

Child's Pose

Kneel on your yoga mat, touching your big toes together beneath you. Bring your buttocks down upon your heels, separating your knees hip width apart. Allow your torso to fold over your thighs as if it were a blanket draped over you, keeping you warm. Relax your torso completely, allowing the gentle curvature of your spine to dictate the position of your arms, which can rest alongside your body or stretch out in front of you. Focus on fully relaxing your body and quieting your mind. Envision your childhood self and breathe into any emotions that arise. Recall the experiences that stripped you of your innocence as you allow memories to wash over you.

My experience as an EYE healer has led me to believe that the way out of emotional pain begins with physical engagement. Motion generates emotion. Our physical experiences on the mat provide a nonverbal mirror, reflecting our lives and ourselves as our bodies see us: as living, growing, worthwhile, and in need of compassion and care. When we dehumanize ourselves, this leads to self-destructive behaviors and torturous addictions – self-cutting, compulsive overeating, cigarette smoking, compulsive gambling, alcoholism, and dozens more. By contrast, when we convert our cognitive chaos into conscious awareness of our bodies, we take better care of ourselves. In fact, by connecting with our bodies, our true self-identities begin to emerge. We accept our feelings without letting our emotions dominate us. Yoga ushers us into our bodies and into ourselves.

Tim's Yoga Experience:

Looking like a cross between the boy next door and an army sergeant, Tim walked with perfect posture and a macho, self-confident swagger. However, the second he stepped onto his yoga mat, his shoulders slumped as if his forty-five years of accumulated life experiences had suddenly pressed down on him.

Tim was clearly burdened by something and, without the inward-looking modality of yoga, would not have been able to give voice to his secret.

"I've never told anyone this, but I'm gay," he confessed after taking Triangle Pose.

Tim opened up about how painful it was for him to pretend to be "straight" for the sake of his bigoted family.

"When I was growing up, my dad called boys like me faggots. My brothers used to beat up the guys who were…" his voice trailed off. His shoulders slumped.

I put my hand on his hip and felt the angle which his body made as I deepened his entry into the posture. "Tell me about your depression," I instructed. "How is it related to your being gay?"

I could feel a shift as his hips began to slacken and some of the tension left his body. It was then that Tim told me about how, in high school, he had taken a bottle of pills and downed half a bottle of vodka because he'd fallen in love with a fellow member of the football team and hated himself for it. He told me about how he hated himself both for being gay and for not being able to own his homosexual identity. He felt like a fraud within his family and in his same-sex relationships.

"Men leave me as soon as they know I'm not going to come out of the closet."

Tim's mother was constantly setting him up on dates with the daughters of her friends. In Triangle Pose, he finally began to realize that he'd been falsely forcing himself into a "straight" posture that was no longer sustainable for him. He began to feel a need to live according to his true identity.

Explore Your Emotions

Triangle Pose

Begin by standing on your yoga mat with your feet about hip width apart. Step backward with your right leg, about 3 to 4 feet, and turn your right foot outward on a 90 degree angle. Align your right heel with the left, tightening your thighs. Keep both legs straight. Bend at the waist to lower your left arm to your left shin, ankle, or to the floor. Stretch your right arm up to the sky and turn your head to look up at your right hand. Keep extension in your legs and torso. Imagine your body is being held between two panes of glass and feel the structure of this pose and the rigidity of the posture. Focus on areas in your life where you feel overly rigid, where you lack flexibility. Focus on maintaining alignment in your body as you tune into feelings of being too controlled. Take Triangle Pose to the other side, again letting your body tell you where you lack spontaneity and joy and how rigidity may be restricting you. Breathe.

Vanessa, Jennifer, and Kristin

What is yoga? The word yoga means "union and discipline." I like to think of yoga as the act of perpetually unifying mind, body and breath. Becoming one with the present moment, again and again, we compress eternity into an instant. When we discipline ourselves to stay on the mat, to keep ourselves and our emotions in the moment, the results can be surprising and transformative. There are many styles of yoga (hatha, vinyasa, ashtanga, iyengar, kundalini, bikram, anusara, jivamukti, forrest, kripalu, integral, sivananda, dahn, power yoga, etc.). Each yogic practice brings its own benefits, arises from its own worldview, and can help in the healing process. My purpose here is not to compare the relative merits of the various types of yoga. The Emotional Yoga Experience is about the effectiveness of release, and it comes from your body and your experiences. One size does not fit all; however, the basic fabric of yoga is intrinsically elastic. As you try on various options, you will no doubt find the one that fits you.

Vanessa's Yoga Experience:

Vanessa had kind eyes, but her smile never reached them. At thirty-seven years old, she was weary of explaining her sadness over a miscarriage that had happened two years before she saw me.

"I'm stuck," she said. "I know what my problems are, but I don't know how to let go and move on."

Later, she described her response to being in Happy Baby Pose as excruciating.

"Even though I never knew my baby, I still loved her. She died inside of me."

Vanessa rocked slowly back and forth, fingers looped around her big toes. Her body shook as she wept and I pressed gently on her thighs, helping her go deeper both physically and emotionally.

She talked about her unborn daughter: "I never knew that it was possible to have a part of you die and to go on anyway."

I held a tissue to her nose and, unabashedly, she allowed me to wipe it. She licked away a tear that had made its way out of one big brown eye, down her cheek to her quivering lips.

"She was unformed inside of me, but somehow formed in my mind. I was going to name her Laurel. Instead, they suctioned her out of me at the hospital."

She told me that she felt as if the best part of her had died when she lost Laurel. More than anything, Vanessa had wanted to be a mother, but she'd decided not to try to conceive again.

"I am too afraid to try again. My husband has stopped asking me about it."

She hugged her knees to her chest and rocked herself gently, as if mothering herself. Then, she offered a poignant image that has imprinted itself in my memory. It is the image that best encapsulates Vanessa, when she first came to see me, before EYE freed her from her grief.

Vanessa described how she had lovingly stenciled the name Laurel on the pale pink cradle that she bought as soon as they knew that they were having a girl. She'd spent hours picking out the right color paint, lovingly laboring over the lettering, interweaving hand-drawn vines and pale pink rosebuds to form her unborn daughter's name. After her loss, Vanessa had moved the cradle into the attic where it remained, collecting dust. A few months before she came for her first session, a violent rainstorm had struck the area and their roof had leaked. Vanessa and her husband, Mark, had gone up to the attic to survey the damage only to discover that the cradle was rain-soaked, the letters had run from the water and it smelled dank and moldy. Vanessa was the physical embodiment of that baby cradle – a once hopeful beacon of life and nurturing reduced by a cruel act of nature.

Explore Your Emotions

Happy Baby Pose

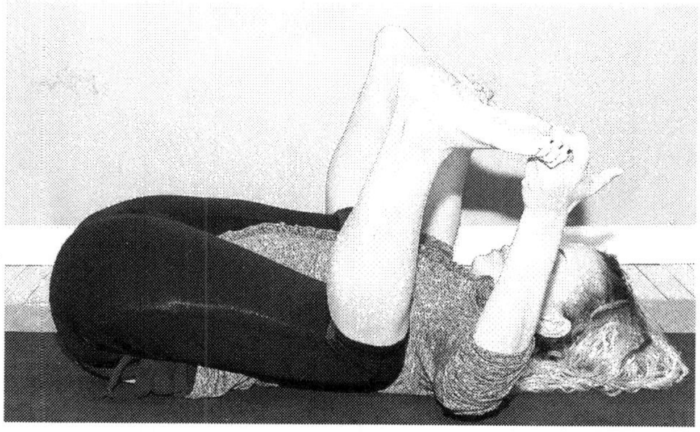

Lie on your back, bending your knees into your belly. Take hold of either the big toes or the outsides of your feet with both hands and open your knees wider than your torso. Flex your feet as you coax your thighs towards your torso and lengthen your spine. Tune in to the sensation of opening in your groin as you focus on feelings of exposure and lost innocence. Breathe into this sensation and allow the vulnerability of your body in this pose to take you into feelings of vulnerability and exposure. Embrace the feelings of exposure, breathing through whatever internal resistance surfaces. Fully experience whatever emotions arise.

The Emotional Yoga Experience transcends traditional talk-therapy making verbal diagnosis unnecessary. It interlocks your physical and emotional experiences. The result is that you transcend your mental limitations and move past your self-limiting beliefs.

For example, you may feel depressed and experience all of the symptoms of clinical depression even though your mind tells you that there is no logical reason for you to be unhappy. The body manifests these feelings and holds onto them until they are released physically. Once the body opens itself to positive energy, both emotional and mental liberation are not only possible; they are inevitable. However, thinking oneself out of depression can be like trying to think away being pregnant. If something is carried in the body, it will transcend the mind. After all, the brain – however important – is only one organ in a body composed of many organs. Because it is the center of reasoning, we mistakenly give it priority in creating and maintaining our body's overall well-being. The body manifests our beliefs and holds our experiences – good or bad, true or false – and that is the mind-body connection that yoga exposes.

Jennifer's Yoga Experience:

Jennifer arrived exactly on time for her appointment. She looked like a Stepford wife – a lovely, thirty-five-year-old blond with blue eyes and a perfect smile. Every inch of her was immaculately coiffed, pressed, and made-up. She was perfect. Even her yoga outfit looked as if it had been ironed! I can't say that I was surprised when she told me that she needed help with her Obsessive Compulsive Disorder (OCD).

In a crisp tone, Jennifer described the rituals that dictated the shape of her day – obsessive checking, cleaning, arranging, hand-washing, and counting. As she stood in Mountain Pose, we both realized that it was the posture that she held 24 hours a day, 7 days a week. Her physically rigid posture mirrored her all-consuming need for behavioral structure. Jennifer was desperate for relief. Despite the fact that she worked hard to maintain an immaculate exterior, her interior was chaos itself. The rules and regulations driving her every action made her feel entirely out of control. Moreover, she was powerless over her disease.

"OCD is destroying my life! But, I can't stop. My husband left me because he can't take my rituals."

Jennifer said her counting, her checking, her routines, and her rituals had been supporting her nearly all of her life. She couldn't remember how or why they had started; however, she knew that they'd been getting progressively worse. The more help she sought, the crazier she felt. It wasn't answers she needed. It was relief! She told me that she'd gotten married at age thirty, but that she and her husband were separated.

"I miss him every day and I know he loves me. But, there isn't room for him and my disorder and I can't give it up. My OCD controls me."

Rather than ask her to analyze her circumstances or to explore her thoughts, I had her stand rigidly in Mountain Pose while breathing deeply and feeling the rigidity of the pose while reflecting upon the rigidity that existed in every area of her life. Her OCD was her way of disconnecting from her feelings and her life. Yoga brought with it a profound sense of connection with herself and her emotions.

Explore Your Emotions

Mountain Pose

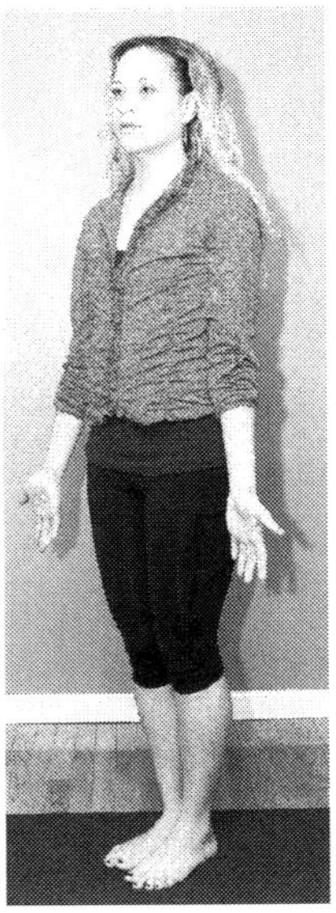

Stand upright on your yoga mat, with your inner thighs pressed together and the sides of your big toes touching, your feet parallel to each other. Balance your weight evenly on both feet. Imagine a long line of energy traveling from your feet up your thighs, through the abdomen, along the spine and out the crown of your head. Imagine your toes as roots, extending into the ground. Your legs, like the trunk of a tree, should be firm. Elongate your back and press your shoulder blades backward, reaching down towards the ground with your hands. Feel the strength of the structure of this pose as you elongate your body. Notice the contradiction between the strength of this pose and the weaknesses in yourself or in your life. Notice what your body is telling you. Hold this pose for several long breaths.

Everyone's body is different, so everyone's path to finding the type of yoga that will work for them will be different, too. The most important elements are physical and emotional awareness. In meditation, we often become aware of emotions as they arise within our bodies and try to express themselves within the silence and stillness that we have created. We attempt to let unbidden thoughts and feelings go as soon as we perceive them, unconcerned about their origins. Yoga differs from meditation because, through yoga postures, we can access specific areas of the body from which specific emotional blockages arise.

Kristin's Yoga Experience:

A walking skeleton, Kristin was emaciated. She came to see me at the direction of her therapist as a last resort before entering a residential eating disorder treatment facility. Fortunately, she never needed it because of her successful work on the mat. It was painful to look at her severely anorexic body. She weighed 87 pounds, and her brain was at war with itself. Half of her was saying that she was the perfect weight, while the other half of her acknowledged that she needed to eat more. Kristin's doctor, therapist, husband, friends, and even her children were deeply concerned about her. Her husband feared that their children would grow up without a mother.

Every day, Kristin made her daughter a grilled cheese sandwich for lunch.

"Why don't you eat, Mommy?" Gina would ask her.

Kristin would reply that she wasn't hungry, which was, paradoxically, the truth. Anorexia had robbed her of the ability to experience the physical sensation of hunger. When she was in Corpse Pose, Kristin's stomach let out a loud gurgling sound. I asked her if she ever wanted her own grilled cheese sandwich and her breathing began to quicken. Fear rose and subsided as she began to acknowledge the hunger that she would not allow herself to feed. She still could not honor her body's messages; however, with yoga, she at least began to hear them.

Explore Your Emotions

Corpse Pose

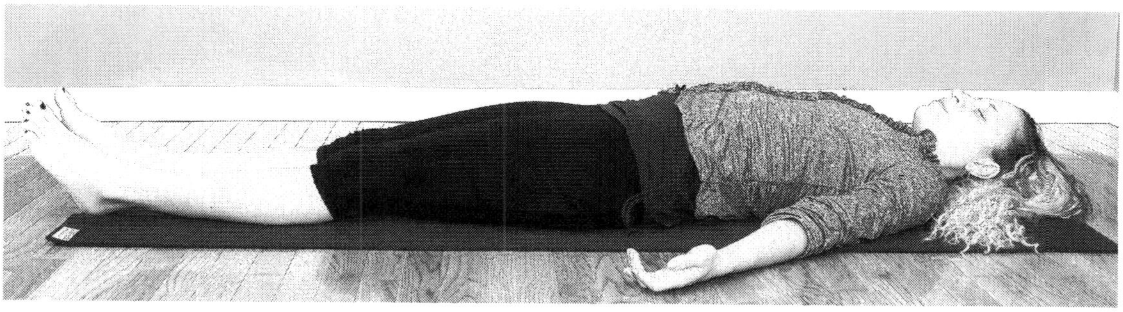

The essential element of this pose is relaxation. Lie on your back, allowing your shoulders to release on the mat and allowing your legs to fully and completely relax. Find a neutral spine. Gradually scan your body for any physical tension and imagine this tension dissipating like a wisp of smoke disappearing into the air. Think about letting go, your body like a corpse, entirely still. This may bring up some intense feelings for you. Breathe into them. Fully feel that which you are holding onto, that which is hard to let go of. Maybe you're clinging to a destructive behavior or person; maybe you're having trouble moving past feelings of grief. Whatever comes up for you, breathe into each emotion, then let it go. Imagine the negative feelings dissipating with each exhalation.

Morgan, Lori, and Maureen

Each of us stores feelings differently because each person's body is different. However, for all of us, emotions are evoked by motion and find their voice during stillness. Strange as it sounds, feelings can be "stored" anywhere – within our skin, bones, joints, muscles, fat, and organs. Our bodies, like our brains, are composed of trillions of cells. The neurons that run through and around them are like sponges, soaking up our experiences. For example, a rape victim may block out the awareness of her physical violation as it is happening. She may not even recall those events afterward because her body has shielded her brain, sparing her from painful memories. Since traumatic memories are harmful, the sub-conscious mind tries to shield her from hurt. However, her body retains those memories, despite its self-protective intentions, and she may experience flashbacks, night sweats, anxiety, and other physical effects from this traumatizing event. The mind can play tricks on us, but the body never does. It continues to love us – to protect itself – even when the mind forgets.

Morgan's Yoga Experience:

A college dropout with a drinking and self-mutilation problem, Morgan only came to see me because her parents had pre-paid for her EYE session. She didn't believe I could help her, or even that she was worthy of healing. Nevertheless, she was willing to try EYE.

"I *know* what happened, but I can't *remember* any of it," she said in a disembodied monotone.

Morgan had told and re-told her story to several psychotherapists and within multiple support groups. She came to our session expecting to tell me the details of what had happened to her. Instead of asking her to access her memories cognitively, I instructed Morgan to submerge herself in her feelings by using her body as an emotional barometer. In Pigeon Pose, she looked inward to find the wisdom within her body.

Every night, Morgan poured her first drink hoping that it would help her to forget what she couldn't consciously remember.

"The first time it happened, I was at a party and I was drunk. I went into a room with him willingly. He was a tall, handsome frat boy. I was a sorority sister. Afterward, when I woke up, he told me I had wanted it. But, I was unconscious. That was the first of an endless rounds of parties and men I can't remember. At college, I became known as the 'drunk whore.'"

A few tears dripped down Morgan's cheeks. She looked at me, her face contorted by her pain. Pulling up the sleeves of her dark grey long-sleeved shirt, she showed me the lines of jagged scars on her arms.

"I cut myself and I drink until I blackout," Morgan confessed.

I could smell a faint whiff of vodka oozing from her pores as her sweat and tears commingled in a noxious, alcoholic odor. Morgan inflicted pain on herself in an attempt to shut out the memories of the pain that had been inflicted upon her by others.

She had been unconscious each time that she was violated. But, that didn't matter. Morgan's body absorbed and retained the pain of her experiences. She felt constant shame.

"At college, they called me the 'drunk whore,'" she repeated.

I asked her what hurt the most. She opened her mouth to say something and, instead, let out a loud sob.

Explore Your Emotions

Pigeon Pose

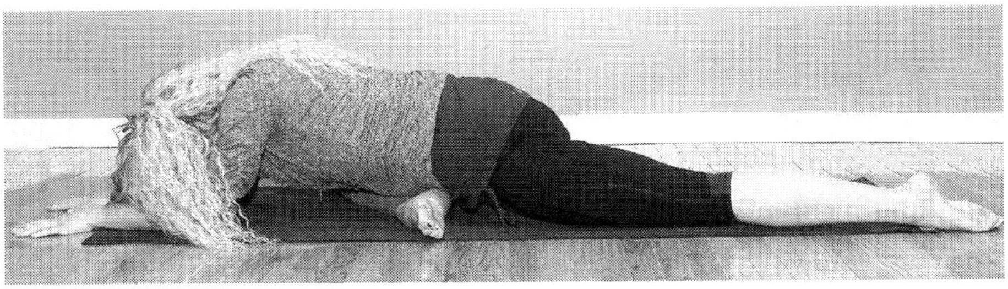

Come into a tabletop position, on all fours with your knees below your hips. Slide your right ankle forward, behind your left wrist. Your right leg will bend and your right shin will be beneath your torso. Stretch your left leg behind you on your yoga mat. Fold forward, allowing the weight of your body over your right leg to intensify the stretch in your right hip. Shame often resides in the hips. As you feel the deep opening in each hip, tune in to your physical and emotional experiences. Go deeper into your shame. After you have fully experienced the hip-opening benefits of this pose, come back to hands and knees and take this pose on the other side. Allow your left hip to have its own voice and its own emotions. Breathe into each sensation. Embrace whatever sins (real or imagined) haunt you. Fully feel the physical and emotional discomfort. Inhale the memory, exhale the emotion. Be with your breath.

Hip openers (such as Pigeon Pose) often evoke deep emotions, especially those having to do with relationships. Since feelings are stored within our body parts, these parts communicate the emotions that have been stuck within them. We can either access our pain directly, through our bodies, or use our feelings to track backwards and identify physical problems. For example, if we find ourselves burdened by a sense of shame the root cause of which we cannot identify, Pigeon Pose may offer a doorway into the source of our guilt. On the other hand, if we are experiencing a great deal of muscular soreness within our hips, we may find (through deeper emotional exploration) that we are harboring unresolved feelings of shame that we were not aware of. Through yogic self-inquiry, after we identify our buried feelings, we may find that some of the physical tension stored within our hips begins to dissipate.

The links between our bodies and our emotions are often less direct than in Morgan's case. Like debris jamming a flood-swollen river, retained emotions clog many natural energy channels. Sometimes, our deep emotional wounds are displayed as chronic physical pain. Other times, the hurts may be imperceptible, evoked only by certain situations. Sometimes, the emotions that we experience are so extreme and so intense that they defy understanding. Have you ever felt unhappy for no reason? Chronic moodiness, even depression, is a sure sign that emotional "debris" is collecting in critical psycho-physical points. The Emotional Yoga Experience demonstrates that, when we use yoga to locate these logjams and apply EFT to clear them, emotional healing results. Through this kind of physiological "archeology," we can delve into long-buried emotions and the emotional experiences that created them. While it may be interesting to unearth the origins of your issues, it is not necessary to know why you feel the way you do in order to release your dysfunctional energy. After all, restoring function is all that really matters.

Lori's Yoga Experience:

Twenty-nine and abuzz with frenetic energy, Lori's entire body twitched spasmodically. She chewed on her fingernails absentmindedly and her legs bounced as if she were a restless child. Unable to sit still, Lori was a bundle of nerves.

"I can't stop twitching. Eek! It's embarrassing."

"Try to stop moving," I instructed her.

"I'm always moving," she laughed nervously.

And it was true. Some part of Lori was always moving. Her legs jiggled. Her fingers fluttered. She vibrated with energy.

Lori looked desperate when I asked her to cultivate stillness, as if she were afraid to slow down, petrified to stop.

"It's a waste of time to 'just breathe.'"

Lori told me that she could breathe as she moved and tried to persuade me that she would benefit from doing Sun Salutations.

"At least then I would be being productive," she said without a trace of irony.

Somehow, I don't think that she understood that the goal of yoga is not to multi-task.

I showed Lori how to fold her body in half while simultaneously looking ahead in Standing Half Forward Bend. Suddenly, the stillness hit her. Almost immediately, her tears flowed.

I watched the weight of all of her emotions drive Lori's body downward, to the floor. She began crying so hard that she couldn't hold the pose anymore. She curled up in a fetal ball on the mat. This time, her body shook with tears rather than with her usual overflow of nervous energy. I wrapped my arms around her, hugging her while she cried.

"What are you feeling?"

"I feel small and insignificant and trapped," Lori's voice cracked. "But I'm also relieved somehow. I want to escape these feelings."

She didn't move. She didn't run from the emotions that surged up within her. Instead, she stayed still and allowed the tears to come.

Explore Your Emotions

Standing Half Forward Bend

Stand on your mat. Bend forward at the waist, lengthening your torso, allowing the torso to meet your legs. Straighten your knees or keep them bent, opening the back of your legs and use your arms to gently pull your torso toward your legs as your head hangs down. Bring the hands to the floor or your shins as you look forward. Envision yourself going inward as you look forward while, at the same, time, looking outside of yourself. Allow your body, rather than your mind, to focus on the internal experience of emotionally "folding in" on yourself. Allow the length of each inhale to match the length of each exhale. Breathe into the stillness.

EYE is only concerned with what works. It provides a surprisingly easy, natural way to access and release feelings contained within the body. This is invaluable for people who have tried conventional talk-therapies (and even nontraditional remedies) and found them lacking. For example, a psychotherapist may spend months, or years, trying to uncover the source of your depression, then take an equally long time trying to help you to talk yourself out of it. How can the same shovel (your mind) that put you in that psychic hole ever dig you out? Instead, let your body *show* you where your subconscious has stored its sad feelings. Ask your body: Where am I holding onto sadness? Or, alternatively, you can ask: Where in my body do I resist joy? Once you tune into your body's answers, you can then excavate and release your pain physically, mentally, and emotionally.

Maureen's Yoga Experience:

A competent career woman whose age I could not discern, Maureen could have been anywhere between thirty and fifty years old. As she strode confidently into our first EYE session, she switched her Blackberry to vibrate. However, once she sat on her yoga mat, Maureen's darting gaze and constant fidgeting revealed a lot of inner turmoil.

"I'm feeling anxious about work," she began. "In fact, I'm in a constant state of anxiety, which is really bizarre because I've been bringing in a lot of new business. All the partners are ecstatic with my performance. Last week, I closed a new account that netted me a five-figure bonus."

As Maureen began to move through a series of yoga poses, her body revealed that she was afraid of not measuring up. Although she knew that her fear was not based on any real inadequacy, Maureen couldn't stop herself from being petrified that her job was in jeopardy.

"I have constant panic attacks about being fired, even though I just got a promotion."

Standing in Warrior I Pose, Maureen's anxiety subsided as a new emotion surfaced.

As she held the pose, I asked her, "What feeling are you fighting not to feel?"

"Loneliness," she told me. "I feel alone."

"How does your anxiety fight off your loneliness? How does your anxiety protect you?"

Immediately, Maureen's right leg began to buckle as realization dawned. Her biggest fear was abandonment. In Warrior I Pose, Maureen was able to link her anxiety with her instinctual need to protect herself against the invasion of even more hurtful emotions. Her biggest fear was of someone penetrating her emotional armor by rejecting her.

Maureen then disclosed her core wound. She had been abandoned by her biological parents when she was still an infant.

"My adoptive family loved me, but I never felt like I really belonged. All throughout my teens and twenties, I went to therapy. I thought I had dealt with these issues. I processed this pain, didn't I?"

I looked at her and we both shook our heads as Maureen gave voice to what we were both thinking.

"No. Apparently, not," she said with a shrug.

Explore Your Emotions

Warrior I Pose

Begin by standing on your yoga mat, feet hip width apart. Step your right leg backward about 3 to 4 feet and turn your right foot out at a 45 degree angle. Bend your left knee to a 90 degree angle while extending your right leg fully. Press downward through your right heel, turning both your right and left hips toward the front of the mat. Extend both arms, reaching strongly upward and lifting your ribcage away from your pelvis. Hold this pose for ten long breaths. As you feel your physical strength, reflect upon areas in your life where you feel weak. Allow your body to tell its story. Breathe. Take Warrior I Pose to the other side. Allow this side its own experience and its own message. Tune in to the moment and feel whatever emotions arise.

Mrs. Walker, Ruth, and C.C.

Our hidden feelings reveal themselves through each Emotional Yoga Experience. You can see the effect even if the cause is unknown. It is like when you flick on a light switch. All that you care about is finding something in a formerly dark space. You do not care who put it there, or how that useful light was generated. This same phenomenon occurs in your body. When your healthy emotional energy flow is turned "off," your mental processes stub their toes in the emotional darkness within your body until you flip the switch that re-opens its energy channels. EYE lights the way to a healthier, happier life. You may or may not ever identify the causes of your negative emotions; however, you will feel so much better that you probably won't even care.

Mrs. Walker's Yoga Experience:

Mrs. Walker, a sixty-seven year old woman, was dying from cancer. She was withering away and was, by her family's accounts, "a mean and bitter old woman."

As her son-in-law told me when I arrived at the hospital to see her, "We're not expecting much. Just keep her comfortable. She's a miserable person and we're hoping that your visit will give us some time off. My wife's about to have a nervous breakdown."

True to form, Mrs. Walker greeted me abruptly.

"Who the hell are you?" she barked when I walked into her hospital room.

"Your daughter and son-in-law asked me to come."

"Oh, you're the girl that does that New Age crap, right?"

"That's me," I smiled.

Mrs. Walker had a lot of anger and certainly wasn't shy about venting her venom at anyone who would listen, including me. Yet, despite her irritability, I liked the crotchety old woman immediately. I showed Mrs. Walker how to do Lion's Breath, which she said made me look ridiculous, but she agreed to humor me since I encouraged her to vent her frustrations between episodes of this yogic breath work.

"I'm not ready to die. I spent my whole life taking care of my ungrateful kids and my cheating husband," she said, sticking out her tongue as she breathed out some of her tension.

"Tell me more about taking care of others," I coaxed.

"There was Rufus, the slobbering dog, and the stuck-up cat. What was her name? Fluffy. That was the ugliest cat I ever saw. I never wanted to get pets, but he'd bring them home from his business trips."

I rolled my eyes upward, stuck out my tongue and let out a "haaa" sound, prompting her to do the same.

"Not that he was doing any business," she continued. "There I was cleaning up cat litter, and he was off to Barbados with his secretary."

Mrs. Walker performed another round of Lion's Breath, this time without prompting. "But, all that is over. I'm too old to get caught up in things that happened almost thirty years ago. Now, I have grandkids I can barely stand and a son-in-law with a beer belly and a voice that gets on my nerves."

She laughed and winked at me conspiratorially. Was the ice around her heart thawing just a bit? I asked her to vent every frustration that she had wanted to vocalize, but never had.

"Haaa," she let loose a torrent of breath. I told her not to hold back, but to let out her anger, frustration, and unarticulated desires.

What emerged was part rant, part roar.

"I never wanted to have kids, but in those days everyone had them. Things were different then. My daughter works forty hours a week and her face always looks like she's been sucking on a lemon. All those wrinkles around her mouth make her look as old as I feel. Sometimes, I catch her on the verge of crying when she looks at me. She knows I'm dying. Her lower lip quivers like it used to when she was a girl and I wouldn't let her get her way.

"I was a good wife and a good mother. I had three kids in four years and wiped noses and butts. I read bedtime stories. I didn't complain when my husband left for work at 7 a.m. and came home at 7 p.m., leaving me to do all the parenting. When our kids were school-aged, I taught other people's snot-nosed kids their ABCs. Then, my husband died while on a 'business trip' in Cancun with one of his secretaries. With our youngest graduating high school, it fell to me to get two kids through college. Tuition was expensive. I got a second job and my hair turned gray.

"I did what I was supposed to do. I got old fast. Now, here I am, sixty-seven years old and dying of cancer. They tell me that I can fight it. I've been fighting my whole damn life and for what? No, thank you. I think I'll lie in this hospital bed and wait for death to take me. My family comes to visit me. 'Perk up,' they tell me. I don't want to perk up. I lived my whole life for other people. Damn all of them! Can't my death at least be about me? I just want to be left alone to die."

Her monologue came out in a rush. Evidently, there was a lot that Mrs. Walker had not said. Her anger covered up years of hurt feelings and thankless sacrifices. Lion's Breath allowed her to access the roaring dissatisfaction that had been coming out as misplaced rage.

Explore Your Emotions

Lion's Breath

Sit in an easy, cross-legged position, your hands resting on your knees. Imagine you're a lion, opening your mouth to roar, baring your tongue and sticking it out. Roll your eyes upward. As you exhale through your mouth, open it wide. Let out a "haaa" sound. Inhale and close your mouth, relaxing your tongue back into your mouth. Come through ten or twelve rounds of Lion's Breath, exhaling a "haaa" and exaggerating the stretch of your mouth as you stick out your tongue, inhaling and relaxing your mouth, then returning the tongue to your mouth and closing your lips. As you do this pranayama (yoga breathing exercise), think about the feelings of frustration and indignance that are escaping your body. Imagine the words you want to roar but do not permit yourself to say out loud. Speak your truth. Feel the power of your own inner roar.

Mrs. Walker's anger ate away at her. Outwardly, she was cruel and vehement. Inwardly, she felt disappointed by her life. Who knows why Mrs. Walker developed cancer? I don't pretend to be a physician and there are so many possible causes of the disease. All I know is that Mrs. Walker had resigned herself to death. At some point, her cancer began to feel like the physical manifestation of years of accumulated dissatisfaction. Lying in her hospital bed, she spent hours reflecting bitterly on the past. Her mind would never have allowed her to go a layer deeper than her anger and to discover the sadness within. Her body articulated this underlying pain.

The physical side of yoga is intensely personal. Remember, motion generates emotion. Various yoga asanas can churn up and release feelings that have been locked within our bodies, providing valuable insights about ourselves and the way we view our lives. Knowing this allows us to choose certain yoga postures to elicit specific emotional responses.

When I first came to yoga, I hated it. In fact, the only reason that I stuck with it was that, in those days, I was a glutton for punishment. I wept during every yoga class. I was angry – at myself, at the teacher, at the world. In the various yoga poses and sequences, I felt fear, sadness, disgust, rage, disapproval, remorse and contempt. Where were the benefits that yoga enthusiasts had talked about? Wasn't I supposed to feel joy, trust, anticipation, optimism, love, and awe? Wasn't yoga the path to true enlightenment?

Initially, I ridiculed myself for these unexpected feelings of weakness and vulnerability. On the mat, my mind played tricks on me. It tried to control something that had a life and a wisdom of its own – my body. My mind told me that if I were doing yoga "correctly" my feelings would change and I would be happy during my practice. However, I continually felt flooded by negative emotions. My fear, sadness, disgust, anger, disapproval, remorse and contempt did not change. What *did* change was my perception of those feelings. Previously, the door to my emotions had been shut. Now, a small crack opened. Through the narrow gap that yoga provided, I discovered that I did not have to conjure or manufacture reality through psychotherapy or with willpower. Instead, I found that truth existed within each breath.

My Yoga Experience:

When I was seventeen years old, I moved in with my boyfriend. He was a drug addict and, when using, was physically, sexually and emotionally abusive. I had blocked out a lot of the events mentally, but through yoga remembered an instance of forcible sex that occurred at a time when I devalued myself and my body. I stayed with an abusive, drug-addicted man simply because he told me he loved me. I ignored any of his behaviors that contradicted his words. Therefore, mentally, I attempted to negate the effect that his actions had on me. However, physically, I held on to the impact of his behaviors.

In Fire Log Pose, my body remembered my violation. Sitting on my yoga mat, I could actually smell the stale odor of pot smoke from ten years before and hear my own faint cries. I acknowledged the pain of that moment as I re-experienced my body. I began to weep. Sitting in Fire Log Pose, my hips released all of the sorrow that my body had retained. For years, I had been so disconnected that I'd been oblivious to these memories or to the pain that they generated within me. Yet, I experienced the impact of this disconnection in the way that I lived my life. Without understanding the causes, I was living with the consequences. I was closed off to intimacy and unable to connect to another person sexually. My body had absorbed the violence that had been perpetrated upon it, both by my ex and by myself. Even though I had blocked out my experience cognitively, I knew the truth physically and experienced it emotionally. My violation affected me deeply. Fire Log Pose opened me up to pain that had been stored within my body, which was impacting my life but of which I had been unaware.

Explore Your Emotions

Fire Log Pose

Sit on your yoga mat in an easy, cross-legged position, hands on knees. Slide your right shin beneath your left shin. Stack your legs on top of one another, right over left. Flex through your feet as you line them up with your knees (your right ankle atop your left knee and your left ankle beneath your right knee). Walk your hands forward, bending over your legs, opening your groin and hips as you fold forward. Your hips can be an area where grief is stored. Let the physical release in your hips excavate memories of losses you have been holding onto like precious, buried treasures. Take Fire Log Pose on the other side, again focusing upon the sensation of opening. Notice if your left hip is holding onto different losses, different griefs than your right hip. Tune in to the story in each hip, allowing each side of your body to articulate its own experience. Trust your body to lead you into and out of your grief.

Emotions arise within the context of experience. However, they may become stuck within the body thereby leaving the mind to create its own way of interpreting reality. Often, emotions are identifiable, although their root causes may not be. For example, when depression appears to have no "cause," depressed people are sometimes told that they simply have a chemical imbalance. Now, I'm not knocking psychiatry, neuroscience, or conventional medicine. I am only saying that, in my experience as both a patient and a healer, I have seen EYE change mental and emotional pathology by directly addressing the bodily anguish that causes them. The Emotional Yoga Experience steps in where the mind and its products – your thoughts – simply weren't designed to go.

Ruth's Yoga Experience:

Perpetual back pain left Ruth feeling like an old woman at fifty-three. Hunched, cavernous shoulders and gnarled and knotted bones brought Ruth to her first EYE session. She dragged herself through my door, grimacing from the pain generated by even simple movements. Ruth had been suffering from physical pain for years and was convinced that her problems were entirely structural and not at all emotional.

She balked when I suggested that she would be best served, at least initially, by doing chair yoga.

"Isn't that for senior citizens? I'm only fifty-three."

Her slumped shoulders and hunched back offered more powerful arguments than anything that I could say. Persuaded by her body, Ruth sat, dispiritedly, and we began.

"My mother always used to tell us to 'Sit up straight,'" Ruth told me. "I used to slump down on purpose. Now, I'd give anything to be able to sit up straight."

Ruth had been seeing a chiropractor for years. She felt tremendous relief immediately following the structural realignment of her spine; however, the adjustments didn't hold. Almost immediately, after each chiropractic session, her body would begin to collapse in on itself again.

Sitting in the chair, Ruth pressed her palms together in Eagle Arms. Her shoulder blades began to spread apart. I put my hands on her shoulders, using my fingers to separate the tension in her muscles. Even as an outsider, I could feel the unmitigated constriction as my hands failed to alleviate the knotted coils of stress surrounding her spine.

Feeling the pressure in her shoulders, I asked, "Where do you feel a sense of pressure in your life? Where do you feel like the weight of the world is on your shoulders?"

It was as if a light bulb went on over her head. Ruth's eyes lit up as realization dawned.

"I am overwhelmed at work. I'm a financial analyst who hates numbers," she told me.

Ruth then went on to say that she never allowed herself to complain about work or to acknowledge the tension that she felt when thinking about her job. Objectively, an outsider would probably have categorized everything about her work situation as ideal. Ruth had a high-powered position at a prominent company, ran a department, and held a great deal of power and prestige within her company. Yet, the story that she tried to tell herself – that she was happy and that everything was okay – was not true.

Interlocking her arms, opening her shoulders, Ruth began to tell a more complete story, "Since I was a child and my mother made me count all of her change every week, so she could take it to the bank and get the cash, I hated money. Now, my whole day is spent hunched over my desk, squinting at my computer screen, looking at numbers. I hate my job!"

Explore Your Emotions

Eagle Arms

Cross your right arm over your left. Intertwine your forearms, and bring your palms together. Bend your elbows, lifting your arms to shoulder-level. Allow your right elbow to snuggle into the crook of the left, like two lovers spooning at night. Feel an opening in the scapula as the shoulder blades spread apart. Feel the pressure of your hands pressing against each other and your arms rising skyward. Allow the physical pressure in your arms and shoulders to evoke feelings of stress within you. After several breaths, reverse your crossed arms, taking this pose again with your left arm crossed over your right. Allow your body to articulate its internal angst. Breathe.

Even though Ruth believed her issues to be purely physical, as soon as she began to do yoga, her body revealed that her emotions were largely responsible for her physical pain. Our bodies often articulate the emotions that we cannot verbalize. They tell a story. It is by observing ourselves in action that we can identify our internal emotional unrest.

Many of my clients come to me for emotional issues only to find that their physical health improves. Conversely, many of my clients come to see me complaining of physical ailments only to discover that their pain has emotional undercurrents. This physical-emotional interplay makes yoga a powerful key – unlocking the entrance to whatever emotions and sensations have imprisoned us.

C.C.'s Yoga Experience:

Enemas and laxatives were ineffective for the thirty-four-year-old client who arrived at my door complaining of intestinal problems. We'll call her C.C. for constipated client.

"I literally feel like shit!" she complained.

C.C. looked like a character from a gothic novel, with raven hair and alabaster skin; however, her pallor appeared to be linked to her digestive problems rather than to her natural coloring. Funny and instantly likeable, C.C. was clever and witty. Although clearly upset by her predicament, she couldn't help but joke about her condition.

"Whoever wrote that book, *Everyone Poops*, lied. I haven't pooped in a week. I look pregnant with a constipation baby. I bet my baby must be 8 pounds, 9 ounces." She rubbed her stomach mockingly and rolled her eyes at me.

"This is crap! I never signed on for this shit." Her words were peppered with references to feces and I wondered if this was subliminal or intentional.

In yoga, twisting poses can stimulate digestion and elimination. I had C.C. lie on her back and hug her knees in towards her torso. She told me that it felt as if someone had tied her intestines into a knot.

"I'm so constipated I can barely bring my knees to the side without feeling like hands are twisting my intestines," she said as she reclined in a Supine Spinal Twist.

I asked her to remember a time in her past when she felt twisted up inside.

"Grade school was a really shitty time for me," she said.

As she lay there, physically twisting her body and feeling impacted and constipated, C.C. told me about the time when Peter Justice, a bullying classmate, punched her in the arm on her sixth birthday and told her that she was ugly.

"My stomach hurt afterward, so I went to the nurse's office."

I asked her if there were other instances of being bullied during her childhood. C.C. brought her knees back to center, then twisted to the other side.

"When was I not bullied? The other girls never invited me to their parties in middle school because I was fat. I spent recess in the bathroom crying. My brother massacred my favorite dolls. I was so upset I threw up all over their headless bodies. He called me a baby and I got in trouble for making a mess. No one gave a crap about me," she told me. "In high school, even my father mocked me for not having a date to the prom. I can still hear his voice telling me 'You really need to get your shit together.'"

Grumbling sounds began to emanate from C.C.'s abdomen. The twisting was clearly churning up more than memories. Waves of muscle contraction in her intestines were beginning to bring movement to her once stagnant bowels.

The links between being bullied and experiencing digestive distress were clear, even if C.C. couldn't yet connect the dots. She got a stomach ache after Peter punched her in middle school, and she sought refuge in the bathroom when the other girls were cruel to her. She threw up all over her headless dolls. For C.C., emotional distress was inextricably linked to her digestion and elimination.

Explore Your Emotions

Supine Spinal Twist

Lie flat on your yoga mat. Bend your knees and cross your right knee over your left. Extend your arms out from your shoulders, resting your palms on the floor, then lower your knees to your left side while turning to look over your right shoulder. Twisting poses promote physical digestion, integration, and elimination. Allow the twisting of your torso to churn up inner angst at your core. Fully integrate these emotions as the opposing rotation of your lower and upper body takes you deeper into the pose and the sensations. Take this twist to the opposite side, with your left leg over your right and your knees lowering to the right side, as you allow your body to bring you deeper into emotional awareness, attempting to digest and eliminate your experiences as you rotate your body.

Tia, Brooke, and Lester

Through each Emotional Yoga Experience, we access subliminal memories, both old and new, and release the pain that they cause. However, even when issues defy rational explanation, we can move past them, because EYE is not a cognitive approach. When the mind is still, the body gets on with the important work of restoring health and harmony without intellectual distractions.

Tia's Yoga Experience:

Tia was a stunning blonde, a Marilyn Monroe look-alike, with startlingly green eyes, high cheekbones and a figure that is best described as voluptuous. Her plunging neckline, peek-a-boo breasts, and luscious curves telegraphed her sexual prowess. Single and smart, she told me that she was generally discontented with her life. Although she didn't have a specific complaint, she had been struggling with emotional wounds for as long as she could remember. In fact, Tia had been in therapy as a pre-teen.

Tia had told her story again and again. When she was six years old, her father began coming into her room at night. The eldest of four girls, she was her father's chosen one. He molested her regularly for years. When she was eleven, fondling and forced oral sex progressed to rape.

"Even though I told him not to, he touched me," she said. "I never told anyone."

Tia had even identified the many ways in which her abusive relationship had led to unhealthy relationships with other men. She knew she dressed provocatively, which added to her sexualization, but she felt her identity was predicated on sex. If she knew this, why was she still trapped in lingering internal angst? Her body held truths that could not possibly be accessed by her mind alone, due to the many filters and judgments that kept her from feeling the true source of her shame.

In Cobbler's Pose, I asked Tia to connect with her sense of vulnerability, to voice her feelings without censorship or judgment.

"Tell me every feeling you had about your father during that time."

She closed her eyes, as if she wanted to shut out the truth. "It's a secret."

I leaned closer as she folded further forward over her legs. Her hair covered her face as if to shield her from her shameful secret.

"I liked it," Tia admitted. "I liked being my daddy's favorite."

She looked at me then, her expression a naked display of vulnerability. For a moment, she didn't look like a 1950s pin-up girl. Instead, Tia resembled an abused puppy – scared and sorrowful.

"I liked what he did to me. He made me feel special. I loved him. I had three sisters and I felt so beautiful when he chose me. That's my secret. Every time he came to my bedroom at night, I felt special. I felt special and ashamed."

Tia had never confronted this duality before because she desperately wanted to hate her father for what he had done to her. Her emotional reality was far more convoluted than her mind wanted it to be and her multi-layered emotions were unacceptable within her world view. Tia's father hurt her, so wasn't she supposed to hate him? On her mat, Tia experienced an upsurge of love beneath the armor of hatred she wore. She told me that she had loved her father and he had loved her. For the first time, she admitted that it had all been incredibly confusing at the time and acknowledged that her emotions were dichotomous.

"I hate to admit it, but I liked being hurt. The truth is that I have never felt as loved as I did when I was with my father." Tia opened her eyes. She was beginning to experience her emotions fully, without censoring them.

I used my hands to press her feet together, which caused her pelvis to open – like a flower blossoming in the spring. I asked her how her relationship patterns as an adult mirrored her childhood feelings of love and longing, hate and hurt.

Her response was as revealing as it was eloquent: "For me, there is something about hurt that feels like love and something about love that feels like hurt."

Through yoga, Tia accessed a different story than she had ever told on a therapist's couch. The events were the same, but her experience of them was different. She had never allowed herself to admit the mixed feelings contained within her body. It was, after all, her body that had surrendered to her father's touch. She disconnected from the opposing emotions within her when she started to tell others about her abuse. They told her that it was depraved, evil, abusive, and criminal. They said that what he had done was bad and that he was a sick person. Objectively, it was wrong and Tia never should have had to endure incest. Yet, she needed to express her feelings about her sexual abuse. Consciously or subconsciously, Tia had told herself that to admit to her love for her father would have made her an accomplice, so she blocked out her "unacceptable" emotions, only accepting feelings she was "supposed" to feel. Eventually, her verbal account obliterated her ability to cognitively access her emotions. Only her body retained the truth. The body she used to get what she wanted was more than a plaything for men. It retained her experiences and she could tune in to its messages.

Still, Tia's cycle of behavior belied the emotional undercurrents flowing within her.

"Since the age of six, I have been searching for the man who will once again make me feel like my daddy made me feel," she told me. "My daddy told me not to tell anyone what he was doing. And I didn't. Then, one day, my mommy sent him away. I never knew what happened, but none of us were allowed to see him after that and I went into therapy for the first time."

In Cobbler's Pose, Tia finally saw that her quest for love and her use of sex to bring herself both pain and pleasure were her ways of articulating her early childhood experiences. It was through yoga that she could fully experience her shame and allow her body to say what her mind had never allowed her to express.

Confused and unsure, Tia said, "I am ashamed because I was hurt and ashamed because I liked it."

Explore Your Emotions

Cobbler's Pose

Sit on your yoga mat, touching the bottom of your feet to one another as if your right and left foot were kissing each other. Draw the soles of your feet apart with your hands, as if they were a book to be opened, keeping the outer edges of both feet on the floor. Allow your knees to splay out to the sides. Bring your heels in as close to your pelvis as you can. Between your knees will be an area of space. Imagine that your pelvis and hip areas (the areas between your knees) are where your vulnerability resides. Allow yourself to get in touch with your feelings of susceptibility, openness, and exposure. Breathe into the physical and emotional discomfort, then bend over this area, allowing your torso to extend forward over your legs. Visualize your torso covering your legs as a metaphor for how in your life you attempt to hide your vulnerability.

Although yoga was the beginning of my own healing journey, it was not enough. The moment that I began to listen to what my body was telling me, I was forced to acknowledge the fact that, emotionally, I was still unraveling – a loose ball of yarn rather than a well-knit whole. My entire body felt like a raw wound – open, vulnerable, and exposed. In the self-destructive cycle of my bulimia, I vacillated between fullness and emptiness, with nothing in between. Notice that neither of these "feelings" are actual emotions. They involve the body sending messages about itself, and I was decoding them all wrong.

Brooke's Yoga Experience:

After her rape two years earlier, Brooke became severely agoraphobic. She refused to leave the house, to meet new people, or even to visit old friends. Her harried mother scheduled her first EYE session, drove her to see me, and then sat in the car for an hour and a half while her daughter began the inward journey that would eventually lead her back to the real world.

When we first met, Brooke seemed to disappear inside the folds of her baggy sweatsuit. She stared fearfully at me with haunted eyes.

"I cry every time I think about what happened," Brooke told me. As if on cue, her eyes began watering. Brooke chewed on her bottom lip to stop it from quivering. "I was walking back to my dorm room late at night. Everything was fine until they came out of the shadows."

I demonstrated Tree Pose, balancing on one leg with my palms in front of my heart. Brooke attempted several times to adopt the pose, only to discover that her balance was off. She kept tilting to one side or another, falling out of the pose.

"Where in your life do you feel unbalanced?" I asked her. "What is it that causes you to lose your sense of balance?"

"I have no balance in my life." Her contempt for herself was palpable. Clearly, Brooke was frustrated by the paralyzing effect fear had on her life. "I never leave the house anymore because I'm terrified of men lurking in dark alleys. I know they are coming for me just like they came for me that night," she told me.

Brooke had been brutally gang-raped on her way back to her college dorm room and suffered from severe Post-Traumatic Stress Disorder (PTSD).

"Does anything bring you back to feeling safe?" I inquired.

"The only time I feel safe is at home, in my bed."

Brooke moved back in with her parents following her harrowing experience. It was as if, in reverting back to childhood, she hoped to protect herself against further violation and obliterate her painful memories.

In Tree Pose, the hood of Brooke's sweatshirt slipped off, revealing short, brutally shorn hair. She told me she'd hacked off her hair herself with a pair of scissors and, each time it began to grow out, she cut it again.

"It used to be long, but I chopped it all off after that night. I got rid of all my fitted jeans and cute shirts and bought hoodies and sweatshirts. I'm scared to look sexy. The new clothes don't help. I'm still afraid."

Her efforts to hide her beauty and disappear within folds of fabric did nothing to restore a sense of balance to Brooke's life or to provide her with emotional and behavioral roots. She felt adrift and unstable.

"This is the first time I've left my house in a year," Brooke said, shaking her head sadly. "I feel off-balance because of the panic inside of me."

I reassured her that I was there to support her physically and emotionally if she needed it. I invited her to hold onto me if she needed to and to use my rootedness to support her in attaining Tree Pose. Yet, Brooke was not yet ready to receive physical support from me. She could not bear to be touched by anyone. So, I allowed her to falter and sway as she experienced the same sensations physically that she lived with emotionally on a daily basis. Brooke was afraid to fall and even more afraid to be caught.

Explore Your Emotions

Tree Pose

Stand on your yoga mat, finding your inner sense of balance. Shift your weight to your left leg, drawing up your right, placing your right sole against your inner left thigh, calf, or ankle (Note: Do not place your foot against your knee as this could potentially injure your knee). Feel your foot against your leg and tune into your body's sense of balance, or lack thereof. Bring your palms together at your heart center, pressing them in prayer position. Balancing poses can be a very effective tool for accessing fear because our physical fear of falling acts as an emotional mirror for that fear. Tune in to the fear that disturbs your sense of equilibrium. Allow yourself to remain in this pose until your balance is challenged and fear surges up from within. Come back to standing on your mat, shifting your weight to your right leg and draw your left foot up along that leg to take Tree Pose on the other side. Take time to notice if a different fear arises or if these feelings of trepidation are the same as before. Breathe into this fear, giving your body a voice, allowing it to stir up the anxiety that exists within you and breathe it out.

Yoga opened me up to the non-verbal language of my feelings. As a novice, I was incapable of going further into the links between my emotions and my body. I knew immediately that yoga was churning things up, the way that a plow prepares fertile ground for planting. Yet, it was only much later, after many years of diligent yoga practice, that I began to realize that different yoga poses elicit different emotions. This new, nonverbal way of exploring the psyche intrigued me, so I became more systematic in my exploration of myself.

Lester's Yoga Experience:

At 6'6," Lester towered over me. Yet, his stature was far from imposing. He was rail thin, as if he subsisted on little more than coffee and self-pity. Lester shook my hand limply. His eyes darted worriedly around the room as he looked anywhere other than at me. A powerful, pungent stench radiated from him, prompting me to recall my past associations with addicts and junkies. Lester had come to see me for anxiety, but, clearly, there was more to it than that.

"I ain't into this yoga shit." Lester was certainly not one to mince words. "I got these anxiety attacks," he told me.

He picked at his dark, mahogany skin, nervously pinching himself. His foot tapped furiously, his breathing was shallow.

I instructed Lester in proper breathing techniques to which he replied, "This breathin' shit is boring."

I smiled at him. I asked him to engage his abdominal muscles in Locust Pose.

"What is at the core of your anxiety?" I asked him. "Visualize your abdominal muscles – your core – as the center of yourself. If your center is overwhelmed by anxiety, ask your body to tell you what it is anxious about."

"I'm just anxious," he said dismissively.

"Is that what your body is saying?" I pressed him to say more.

"No," Lester admitted.

"What is your body saying?"

"My body is wanting something to take the edge off my anxiety." He glanced nervously around the room, having no intention of admitting his addiction. I knew not to force the issue. His body had a story to tell and it was speaking to him. Whether or not he chose to tell me what it said was a different matter entirely.

"What is the feeling behind your anxiety?" I asked him.

"I ain't got no control," Lester told me. "I can't explain the feeling. But, that's what it is. I got no control. I'm a grown-ass man and I can't control nothing."

I asked him to tell me more about where he felt out of control in his life.

"I worked all my life, took care of my brother, my mother, and my li'l sister. I took care of all of them. And I shouldn't of had to do none of it. I had to be the man of the house when I was just a boy myself." He kept talking, telling me about his anxiety, about how he felt as if he had lost his core sense of self when he had to assume adult responsibilities as a child.

Then, Lester surprised us both by saying, "I got a problem with coke. I'm an addict."

Lester had never admitted his addiction before – either to himself or to anyone else. For him, the physical act of yoga disarmed his mental resistance to expressing his drug addiction.

Explore Your Emotions

Locust Pose

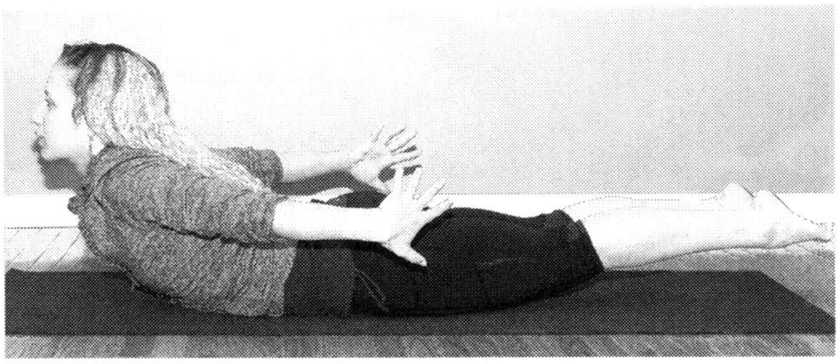

Lie face down on your yoga mat with your legs extended. Point your toes and feel your abdomen press into the earth. Rest your arms alongside your body, by your hips, palms facing one another. Lift your torso, legs and arms, simultaneously elongating your body as you lift. This is a core-strengthening pose, tapping into your abdomen and unearthing deeply held, "gut-level" feelings and experiences, freeing you to acknowledge emotions that exist at your core. At your center, there are feelings that drive you, dictating your actions and reactions. Hold this pose, allowing your abdominal muscles to engage and heat to build in your body. The muscles in your belly and back may begin to tremble as emotions build and you energize and strengthen your core. Try to breathe even as you engage your abdominal muscles.

Margaret, Samantha, and Beth

Ask any yoga teacher to tell you about his or her students' emotional releases during class and you'll likely be flooded with stories about sobs, sighs, and even primal screams. These emotional shifts may be subtle or intense, expressed outwardly and dramatically, or internally (as part of a student's personal growth). However, all of these reactions, overt or subtle, have a ripple effect. I first realized this when I began doing yoga on my own without instructors or classmates looking on. However, from attending and teaching yoga classes and speaking to other yogis, I realized that my experiences were not unique. Everyone's body stores feelings and yoga provides a powerful escape hatch for these emotions.

Margaret's Yoga Experience:

Margaret was completely shut down. Scheduling her appointment on the phone, her voice was a detached monotone. Even though Margaret had emigrated from Britain to the United States in order to marry her American-born husband, even though she had built her life according to his needs and whims, and even though he had repeatedly been unfaithful to her, she told me matter-of-factly that she had gotten over her ex-husband's infidelities. During her EYE session, however, Margaret's body told an entirely different story.

Originally from London and having lived in the U.S. for ten years, her accent was still as thick as Yorkshire pudding. Cultivated and proper, her voice was rich in tone and texture. Margaret spoke in allegories, and regally rolled her r's.

"I quite fancy the Lion from the *Wizard of Oz.* Silly bloke went looking for a heart and found he had one all the time," she told me.

As she opened her chest physically in Sphinx Pose, her metaphorical heart expanded simultaneously. Margaret told me about how she came here to get married. She had given up everything in order to immigrate and had centered her life around her husband. Then, two years before her EYE session, she had walked in on her husband in bed with another woman.

After catching him red-handed, Margaret had been shocked to discover that his infidelities had been systematic and ongoing. She had filed for divorce immediately.

In Sphinx Pose, Margaret described the sensations that she experienced as the melting of her solid exterior.

"I could become a puddle. I could melt right here, leaving nothing behind but my clothing on this yoga mat," she said as she described how painful it had been to have her hopes and dreams destroyed. "Back home, when I was a baby-minder, I'd dream of moving across the pond. My ex was quite the charmer and I believed all of his lies. In the end, he was a royal wanker."

Something internal shifted for Margaret while in Sphinx Pose. It was painful for her to connect with her emotions, since she had shut them off immediately following the discovery of her ex's infidelities. However, hope surfaced too. It mixed with her pain and renewed her ability to connect with her emotions.

"I feel like I am coming back to the person I used to be. When I was young, I believed in love. I wore white on my wedding day. I gave up my dream of having children because my husband didn't fancy being a father. I moved to the States for love. Then, after he had a leg over with that woman, my world fell apart. I lost everything. I signed the divorce papers and closed my heart."

Margaret connected with her anger, her hurt, and her profound sense of longing and loss. Her tears provided a wave of relief.

Then, in a testimony to her brilliance and self-mocking sense of humor, she circled back to her previous reference about the *Wizard of Oz:* "I guess I, too, have a heart," she said with a wink.

Explore Your Emotions

Sphinx Pose

Lie on your abdomen. Squeeze your right and left thighs together. Lengthen through your spine and rotate your thighs inward. Prop your elbows under your torso while keeping both forearms on the floor. The arms should be parallel to one another. Lift your torso and head off the floor, bending your back slightly. Keep your forearms pressing firmly downward to create more lift in your torso. Look skyward while pressing downward through your forearms, hands and legs while pointing your feet directly behind you. Feel your chest opening and the muscles encasing your heart spreading. Feel your shoulder blades pulling backward, away from one another. Breathe in this heart-opening pose. Feel the opening of your chest and the expansion of your heart as you identify whatever internal and external barriers are keeping you from giving and receiving love.

Our physical selves reflect our emotional selves. A dancer moves with poise and grace. A depressed person slumps, shoulders hunched, eyes downcast. A child skips happily. Our bodies reinforce and express our moods, even when we can't articulate them. In other words, our bodies wear our emotions. If you get drunk, you will spend the next day bleary-eyed and hung-over. If you get a massage, you will move with greater ease and energy. If you eat food out of unhappiness or compulsion, you will wear those feelings and behaviors as excess weight.

Samantha's Yoga Experience:

Layers of cascading fabric draped over Samantha's flabby, formless body. She came to see me because she wanted to lose weight. From my window, I watched her devour a donut as she walked from her car towards my door. She paused, momentarily, to reapply her lipstick, before ringing my doorbell.

When she sat down on her yoga mat, rolls of belly fat bunched up around her and she self-consciously crossed her arms in front of her in an effort to hide her body. Even though she was incapable of modifying her food intake, Samantha was scathingly contemptuous of her body and her weight.

"How did I get to be so fat? I look like a sumo wrestler," she said.

Easy Pose did not feel easy for Samantha.

"This yoga mat disappears under the folds of my ass-fat," she told me.

At nearly 300 pounds, Samantha struggled with a profound disconnect between her mind and her body. She craved food constantly even though, mentally, she wanted to change. Samantha confessed to a love affair with donuts and to perpetual dieting failures.

"My mouth still tastes like powdered sugar and, already, I'm daydreaming about hitting the Dunkin Donuts drive-through on my way home," she said honestly, shaking her head in puzzlement at the incomprehensibility of her own compulsive eating behavior. "I can't believe that I am thinking about food again. How did I become this person? I look like the before picture for a diet commercial."

However, self-recrimination is the purview of the mind and I told Samantha to "stop thinking and start feeling."

In Easy Pose, I asked her to connect with a memory of a time when she felt safe and to conjure up that image of safety. I asked her when she had felt a sense of ease in her life.

Samantha realized, suddenly, that she never felt safe except when she was putting something into her mouth. For her, food acted as her defender and her excess weight provided her with emotional insulation. In fact, looking at her, I could see all of the physical barriers that Samantha had built between herself and the world. She wore loose, multi-layered garments that looked more like drapery than clothing. Her makeup had been heavily-applied – caked on in layers of powder and paint. All of the layers of fat draped around her made Samantha feel protected.

"My food and my fat keep me safe," she realized.

Explore Your Emotions

Easy Pose

Sit on your mat. You may want to put a folded blanket or a yoga block underneath your buttocks for comfort. Cross your legs, slipping one foot in front of the other, and place your feet below your knees. Ideally, your knees will come below your hips. Keep your head and body straight, close your eyes and breathe deeply, bringing breath into your belly. This is a pose of surrender, ease, and stillness that often leads to tremendous awareness as you gaze inward and use the stillness of your body to receive the messages it is giving you. Experience whatever feelings of physical or emotional unrest surge up from within you. Invariably, your body will speak to you. Your job is to be still long enough to hear what it is saying. Listen to your body.

Samantha's experience demonstrates the value of looking to our body for answers. The nonverbal aspects of yoga reveal the connection between our physical forms and our feelings. The body retains our emotional truths and communicates them as layers of fat, chronic disease, persistent pain, or a host of other major or minor complaints. Listen to what your body is telling – and showing – you.

Beth's Yoga Experience:

A fifty-six year old mother and grandmother, Beth came to see me to deal with her depression and anxiety. Her body revealed a deeply-held conviction that she had failed at her most important role – motherhood.

Beth had been doing yoga for years and told me that she loved it. Thin and wiry, she possessed the quintessential yoga-body.

"Yoga always makes me feel so good," she gushed. "I mean, I am majorly depressed about life, but then I do it and I feel so great during every class. If I could just spend all day doing yoga, I'd be happy."

She then proceeded to rattle off the names of all of her favorite yoga poses – Child's Pose, Downward Dog, Chair Pose, Pigeon Pose, Standing Forward Bend, Warrior I, Triangle Pose, Boat Pose... The list seemed endless. Yet, I noticed immediately that none of Beth's "favorites" included back-bending or heart-opening poses. I asked her about this.

"Oh, I don't like those," she told me. "I don't like how they make me feel, so I don't do them."

Interested, I inquired further. "Do you mean how they make you feel physically? Do you have any injuries?"

"Oh, no. They make me cry and I do yoga to feel good, so I just avoid them," Beth said nonchalantly.

So guess where I had Beth begin? With backbends. As she bent her body backwards, I invited Beth to look back into her past experiences. I asked her what memories she avoided recalling. As soon as she lifted her pelvis in Bridge Pose, the waterworks turned on. Through her tears, Beth told me about her daughter, Julia, and how, at age eleven, Julia had told her mother that she hated her.

"I cried myself to sleep that night. I know kids say mean things to their parents all the time, but I couldn't let it go like other parents can. I took it personally. I'm too sensitive."

Clearly, Beth had absorbed her daughter's words and had been wounded by them. She couldn't seem to move past her belief that her daughter hated her. Intellectually, she knew that Julia loved her, but, emotionally, she was fixated on her own perceived failures.

What's more, Julia was now a grown woman with a daughter of her own. Beth's deep-seated belief in her own inadequacy had persisted for years and had only grown more pronounced over time, causing her to doubt her granddaughter's love for her as well as her daughter's proclamations of affection.

"My granddaughter is beautiful. Sasha always says she loves her 'Nana.' And I love her, but I still don't feel like I measure up."

Beth desperately tried to compensate for her feelings of inadequacy to no avail.

"No matter how much money I send my daughter every month, no matter how often I babysit Sasha, I never feel good enough."

Without being cognitively aware of her pattern, Beth had been trying to ingratiate herself to her daughter ever since Julia uttered those harsh words in a fit of rage when she was just eleven years old. Beth hadn't even recognized that her depression had any connection with her roles as a mother and grandmother. In fact, anyone who knew her would have said she derived tremendous joy from her relationships with her daughter and granddaughter. Yet, Beth's body told a more complex story – one of a woman's desperate attempts to prove her lovability despite her chronic feelings of worthlessness.

In Bridge Pose, I asked Beth to feel the sensation of bending over backwards for others just to prove her worth. After several breaths, she was so physically exhausted by the pose that she lowered down out of it. Bridge Pose provided a mirror in which Beth could see her behaviors and emotions reflected back at her.

"I'm exhausted by trying to be the best mother I can be. It's never enough," Beth told me.

As she lowered out of the pose, she began to cry. Her tears swept through her body in a tidal-wave of grief. Beth described the feeling of sinking onto her yoga mat as being akin to the sinking sensation she felt at not measuring up to her daughter's expectations. For twenty-four years, Beth had been replaying her daughter's words, re-experiencing her hurt over and over again. Bridge Pose was like pouring antiseptic on her wounds – it stirred up her pain even as it began her healing process.

Explore Your Emotions

Bridge Pose

Lie on your back on your yoga mat with your knees bent and your feet resting on the floor, your heels as close to your buttocks as you can comfortably get them. Bring your arms to rest alongside your body. Press your palms and feet down firmly as you push your tailbone upward, lifting your buttocks off the floor while keeping your thighs and feet parallel. Keep your arms pressing down alongside your body as you lift your pelvis high. Holding this pose requires a great deal of strength and focus. As you hold this backbend, focus on the physical sensation of exhaustion and weariness. Reflect upon areas in your life where you've felt exhausted by extending yourself for others or "bending over backwards" on behalf of another person. Breathe into the discomfort until it dissipates, then slowly lower your spine to the mat, one vertebra at a time. End by hugging your knees into your chest.

Digging Deeper: Putting it Together, Using Yoga to Explore Your Emotions

So what types of emotions does our body hold and where does it hold them? How can we access these internal snarls and sensations through yoga?

Based on my own personal healing, client experiences, and research into the mind-body connection, I created the following chart as a useful tool for inward-looking yoga. Use it as an experiential and diagnostic guide. If you feel any physical discomfort in the following areas of your body, or experience any persistent emotional unrest for reasons you can't explain, try one of the corresponding yoga poses. Let your body tell its story and listen to what it says.

Body Part(s)	Emotion(s)	Yoga Pose(s)
Head and Face	Anger Contempt	Lion's Breath (page 16) Headstand
Neck	Fear Anger	Fish Pose (page 118) Net-Bearer Bond
Eyes	Surprise Awe Sadness	Note: Focusing on the third-eye during any yoga posture
Throat	Fear Surprise Love Submission Remorse Disgust	Fish Pose (page 118) Net-Bearer Bond
Heart and Chest	Love Anticipation Joy Trust Optimism	Cat Pose (page 81) Cow Pose (page 81) Cobra Pose Bridge Pose (page 28) Wheel Pose (page 119) Fish Pose (page 118) Camel Pose (page 118) Sphinx Pose (pages 26 and 97)

Body Part(s)	Emotion(s)	Yoga Pose(s)
Arms and Shoulders	Anticipation Fear Aggressiveness	Eagle Pose (page 18) Crane Pose Plank Pose (page 93) Downward Dog (pages 5 and 86) Dolphin Pose
Belly and Abdomen	Trust Fear Sadness Disgust Anger Anticipation Disapproval Remorse Contempt Surprise	Cat Pose (page 81) Cow Pose (page 81) Cobra Pose Bridge Pose (page 28) Wheel Pose (page 119) Fish Pose (page 118) Camel Pose (page 118) Boat Pose Sphinx Pose (pages 26 and 97) Locust Pose (page 24) Note: Breath of Fire is helpful to access these emotions. (page 87)
Diaphragm and Waist	Fear Sadness Anger Remorse Contempt	Seated Forward Bend Standing Forward Bend Gate Pose (page 118)
Pelvis and Hips	Joy Trust Anticipation Optimism Love Submission Disapproval Aggressiveness	Bound Angle Pose Fire Log Pose (pages 17 and 85) Bridge Pose (page 28) Upward Dog Pose (page 93) Pigeon Pose (pages 12 and 83-84) Wide Angle Seated Forward Bend Happy Baby Pose (page 9) Frog Pose (page 118)

Body Part(s)	Emotion(s)	Yoga Pose(s)
Legs	Fear Trust Sadness Surprise	Tree Pose (pages 23 and 89) Staff Pose Dancer's Pose (page 90) Chair Pose Mountain Pose (page 10) Warrior Poses (I, II, and III) (page 14 — I only) High Lunge
Back and Spine	Joy Fear Optimism Awe Disapproval Remorse Contempt	Cat Pose (page 81) Cow Pose (page 81) Downward Dog (pages 5 and 86) Upward Dog (page 93) Locust Pose (page 24) Seated Forward Bend
Joints	Joy Trust Sadness Love Submission Disapproval	Hero Pose Reclining Hero Pose (page 119) Crow Pose Plank Pose (page 93) Half Moon Pose
Bones	Trust Fear Love Submission Awe	Corpse Pose (page 11) Mountain Pose (page 10) Sun Salutations Triangle Pose (page 7)

We find a direct link between yoga poses and our emotions. Even after an emotional breakthrough occurs, the repeated practice of yoga becomes a ritual expression of the reunited self, a way of fusing the mind and the body within a given, timeless moment. Yoga builds self-awareness. It is a beautiful, artful way to invoke healing and is the first step toward true and lasting wellness. Yoga brings us out of our minds, with all of its self-deceptions, and into our bodies, which never lie. It unearths long-buried emotions from the body. Like buried treasure, these suppressed feelings require a map to locate. Yoga pinpoints the location of our blocked energy as it explores beneath the surface, digging deep.

As the first step in the healing process, yoga reunites us with the moment. Breathe deeply. Experience the yoga. The next step is Emotional Freedom.

Equalize: Use EFT to Balance Your Body's Energy

Have you ever been stuck indoors at night during a power outage? Have you sat, terrified and trembling in the dark, while a storm ensued outside? One second, the lights were on; you could see clearly no matter what elements were raging outdoors – rain, thunder, lightning, snow, or wind. The next instant, darkness enveloped you, leaving you suddenly incapable of doing or seeing anything. Nothing worked – not the television, the fridge, or the radio.

Getting stuck in a negative emotional state feels like being trapped in the dark during a power outage. Just as you are unable to turn the lights on until power is restored, it is impossible for you to feel positive emotions until your body's energy system has been reset. Once this repair occurs, however, feeling good becomes as effortless as flipping on a light switch.

You may be wondering: How does this apply to EFT? What is the Emotional Freedom Technique, and how does it work? The Emotional Freedom Technique (EFT) reconnects the emotional wiring in our physical bodies. It brings energy back to the body like a technician routing power back to your house after everything has gone dark. To continue the metaphor, EFT turns on the lights in the dark room of your emotions.

Without explaining the science and methodology behind the technique, I will tell you that EFT is supported by countless examples of people whose lives have been immeasurably improved by this simple, but effective, approach to emotional wholeness. Combining ancient methods with more recent, cutting-edge research, EFT utilizes both modern and traditional wisdom. The same principles behind the ancient Chinese system of acupuncture inform and impact EFT. If you have ever been to an acupuncturist's office, you have probably seen a chart of the human body with various colored lines mapped onto the body in a series of intersecting lines. These lines trace routes of various energy systems, also known as meridians, up and down the body. The energetic meridians each have their own pathways, which act as invisible conduits of energetic flow. There are many points along each meridian which can be used to unblock the places in your body where your energy has become stuck.

That explains why, if you have ever had acupuncture, you may have noticed that the site of your problem may not be the location where you receive treatment. For example, if your complaint is a headache, you may end up with needles in your legs or arms or ears (not, as you might expect, your head). This is because each meridian connects seemingly disconnected parts of our bodies along an intricate energy system. This same connectivity is what makes EFT effective. Just like the acupuncturist's needle piercing the skin, EFT works on the body's energetic pathways. The good news is that EFT won't require you to learn any of the intricate science behind these connecting energetic pathways or to identify the places where your energy is stuck, nor will you need to stick yourself with needles or pinpoint the places in your body where the disruption in your energy has occurred.

Yes! You can breathe a sigh of relief. EFT is painless and unobtrusive and there are no adverse side-effects. It is an extremely non-invasive approach to healing which involves gently tapping on various points on your body. EFT requires that you tap near the end points of your energy meridians. As you gently tap on your body, knocking on the door to your feelings, you will find that the door swings open and positive emotions invite you inside. It might help to think of EFT as a sort of needle-less emotional acupuncture.

Founded by Gary Craig, an engineer, EFT is an effective and results-oriented approach to feeling good. Like any competent scientist, Craig developed his methods based on empirical evidence. He wanted to find an effective technique for treating emotional issues which produced positive results quickly and easily. The miracle of EFT is that, when used correctly, it *resolves* physical and emotional issues rapidly and permanently.

Gary Craig states that EFT is based upon the following premise: "The cause of all negative emotions is a disruption in the body's energy system." Practically, what this means is that, often, when something happens, the energy of the body is interrupted and a negative emotion results. Thus, emotional dysfunction is body-based, stemming from faulty internal wiring or blown internal circuitry. As you use EFT to correct the problem, you will release your blocked energy and your negative emotions will vanish.

As an example to illustrate how this works, let's imagine two people are walking along together when, in front of them, a fatal car accident occurs. Naturally, both people will feel an immediate emotional response: shock, dismay, fear and a host of other emotions. However, then what? Maybe one of them will suffer an energetic shutdown and be left unable to function – operating in a constant state of fear and crippling anxiety for months after the incident. Whatever energetic jolt occurred, this person becomes stuck in fear. The other witness to the same event may move on relatively quickly and be virtually unscathed by the incident. Both people witnessed the exact same accident, yet their responses were entirely unique. What's the difference? The energetic interruption. The divergence between their reactions has nothing to do with *experience*. It resides within the body's energetic response to events. This explains why two people can grow up in the same dysfunctional household and one will emerge well-adjusted while the other emerges burdened by negative emotions.

What about the mind's role in all of this? How about talking yourself out of negative feelings? With EFT, attempting to alter your thoughts as a way of changing your emotions becomes unnecessary. Asking someone to try to think their way from negative to positive emotions is like asking them to turn on a light switch connected to a blown bulb. Positive emotions can't occur because, until our internal electricity is repaired, our energy can't turn on the lights of our emotions. With disconnected circuitry, our energy can't flow freely. Once the energy is flowing again, positive emotions are not only possible, they are inevitable.

With EFT, the relief provided is energetic! Because EFT corrects the body's energetic upset, it works equally well no matter the magnitude of the issue or the emotional attachment. It can effectively treat depression, Obsessive Compulsive Disorder (OCD), anxiety, guilt, anger, Post-Traumatic Stress Disorder (PTSD), addiction, grief, loneliness, chronic and acute physical pain and a multitude of other issues. Within minutes, the body's energy system can be revitalized, energetic equilibrium restored, and negative emotions will vanish.

Although there are various levels of complexity with EFT sequencing, the following is a simple, but effective, version of EFT which works according to a three-step process:

The Setup.
The Sequence.
Repeat the Sequence.

The Setup

This is the critical first step in the Emotional Freedom Technique. It is here that you prepare your body's energy system for the removal of energetic disruptions. The setup calls attention to your existing emotional state while also helping to release your self-destructive thoughts and feelings. It is an affirmation of sorts; however, it works differently than many other affirmations that you may have tried.

The EFT affirmation, unlike other affirmations, begins with acknowledging the problem. Have you ever attempted to repeat positive affirmations to yourself with little or no result? I have looked in the mirror and told myself "You are beautiful," only to have the little voice in the back of my head emerge and tell me, "You're wrong. You're not beautiful." When we are conditioned towards negative self-talk, our brains discount positive affirmations. EFT considers our negative thinking and combats self-defeating interference by anticipating these human tendencies towards negative self-talk and counteracting this energy in advance. While traditional, positive affirmations try to repress negative thoughts and deny negative emotions, EFT acknowledges them upfront. The body is wise. It doesn't like being lied to. To say "Even though I have this (insert negative emotion or behavior here), I deeply and completely love and accept myself," recognizes the negative undercurrents contained within your body. You acknowledge your truth even as you transcend it.

To begin setting your body up energetially for positive transformation, tap the Karate Chop Point (located on the side of your hand) continuously while repeating the EFT affirmation three times out loud and focusing upon your problem or emotion. The Karate Chop Point should be tapped vigorously with the full side of the hand tapping the other hand (hence, the name "Karate Chop"). Repeating this neutralizing affirmation (the setup phrase) will lay the foundation for your body's energetic reset.

Karate Chop Point

Karate Chop Point

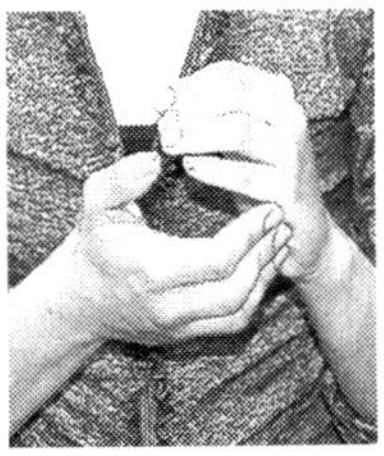

So, if you are struggling with deep-seated anxiety that is interfering with your life, you would say, "Even though I have this crippling anxiety, I deeply and completely love and accept myself." Or, if you are depressed about your financial situation, you might say, "Even though I feel depressed over my financial situation, I deeply and completely love and accept myself."

The Sequence

The tapping sequence is designed to unblock stuck energy from the body and then to release it. Repeat the reminder phrase (the same word or words that you inserted into the underlined phrase) while tapping on the following points in the following order. For example, you might say "this crippling anxiety" or "this depression about paying my bills." Tapping on the end points of your energetic meridians, while focusing on the problem and repeating the reminder phrase, provides an energetic tune-up. The energy is unblocked and negative emotions dissipate.

Tap the points in the sequence outlined below. Do so with slight pressure, but not to the point of pain. Use two fingers to tap. I suggest tapping on both sides of the body simultaneously, using both your right and left hands, to achieve maximum effect. This is not a necessary EFT practice; however, it ensures a more comprehensive approach to energy-balancing and thereby accelerates your healing process.

Repeat The Sequence

Repeat the tapping sequence (outlined below), careful to repeat the reminder phrase while tapping down the body along the points in the order given. Remember to tap on each of the energy points given below while repeating the **Reminder Phrase** (the issue) at each point. Tap as long as it takes to repeat the phrase once then move on to the next point.

EFT in Action:To Perform EFT, Follow the Sequence Below

The Setup... Repeat the setup statement three times while continuously tapping the Karate Chop Point.

"Even though I have this problem with (state the issue), I deeply and completely love and accept myself."

Karate Chop Point

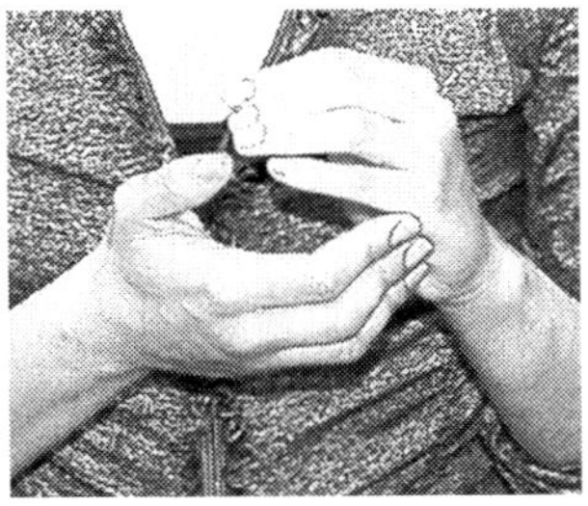

The Sequence H, EB, SE, UE, UN, CH, CB, UA … Tap continuously on each of the following energy points while repeating the ***Reminder Phrase (the issue)*** at each point. Tap as long as it takes you to repeat the phrase once, then move to the next point.

H-Crown of Head

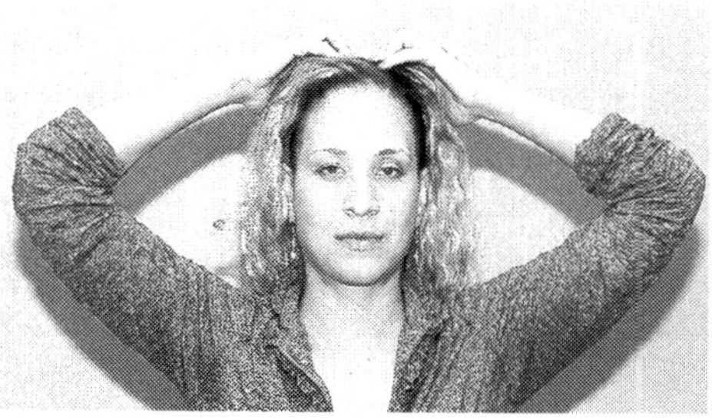

EB-Eyebrow

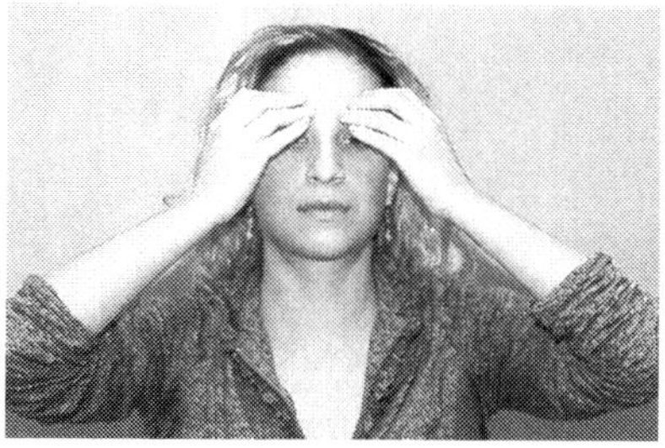

SE-Side of Eye

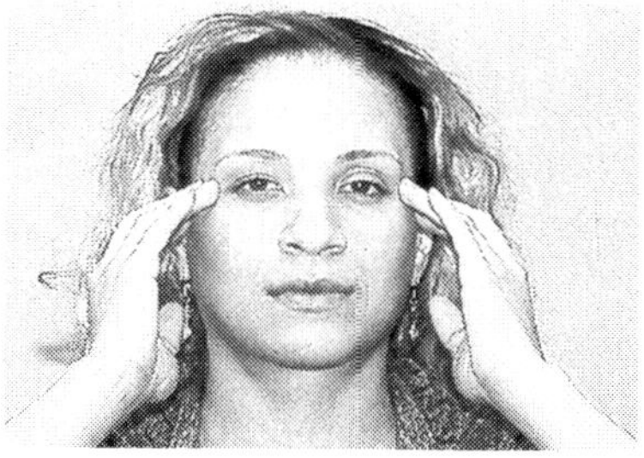

UE-Under Eye

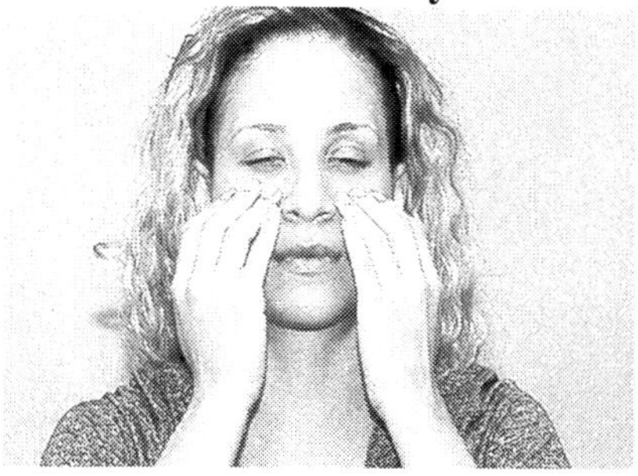

UN-Under Nose

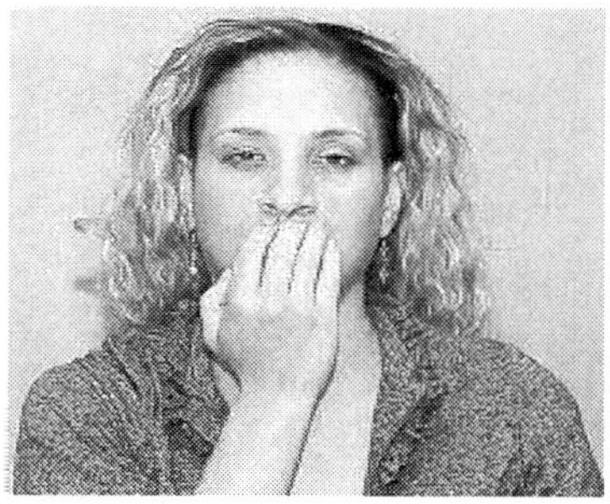

CH-Under Chin

CB-Collar Bone

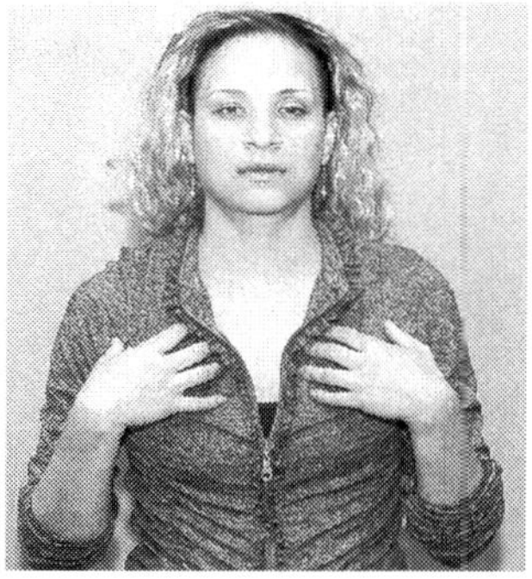

UA-Under Arm

Repeat The Sequence H, EB, SE, UE, UN, CH, CB, UA …

One more time, tap continuously on each of the above-given energy points while repeating the ***Reminder Phrase (the issue)*** at each point. Tap as long as it takes you to repeat the phrase once, then move to the next point.

As you can see, EFT asks that you identify your issue and then perform **The Setup, The Sequence,** and **The Sequence** again, thereby balancing your emotional attachment to an issue and negating whatever emotional charge you feel related to a given situation.

How can you use EFT to balance your energy system? By focusing in on your problem while tapping on the end points of your body's energy meridians, you will release and unblock old issues. That doesn't mean, however, that you can stop reading here or that, now that you have learned EFT, you can apply it as an emotional cure-all. Why not? Just as yoga can diagnose emotional issues, but lacks the power to resolve them, EFT can heal emotional issues, but is often inadequate as a diagnostic agent.

Typically, a conventional EFT practitioner uses talk-therapy to diagnose a client's issues. A person seeking help with resolving the emotional issues that he or she can identify and express presents his or her experiences to a practitioner. This process requires a certain pre-existing level of self-awareness. Clients are expected to be able to identify the source of their energetic disruption cognitively, and to express it verbally. This is inherently problematic. In my work as an EFT practitioner, it has become abundantly clear to me that, when dealing with emotional issues, our minds often impede, rather than accelerate, the healing process.

You have probably heard the old joke about cognitive therapy: How many therapists does it take to change a light bulb? Only one, but the light bulb has to really want to change.

While this joke may be amusing, being unable to change is discouraging and demoralizing. In my experience, even people who want to alter themselves frequently can't despite all of their best intentions. Often, even in the face of dire consequences, emotional anguish, and an inner desperation to be different, change remains elusive. I, myself, was such a hopeless case. Even the most qualified conventional treatment providers and widely-endorsed modalities made little or no progress towards reducing my bulimic symptoms. Insights abounded, but change remained impossible.

People wanting to cognitively understand their issues often identify the problem only to find themselves still unable to heal emotionally or behaviorally. Why the disconnect? Because the mind cannot restore emotional balance. The disruption in your body's energy system *causes* your disturbed emotions. The brain cannot repair your internal circuitry because the body is the source of your distress and, therefore, must also be the source of your healing.

I am a huge believer in the power of EFT because I have seen it work and felt its benefits firsthand. I came to EFT because I wanted to change and felt incapable of doing so. My eating disorder was out of control and I was miserable. My life was literally going down the drain (a bit of bulimic humor). I had intended to go to a hypnotherapist, thinking that she might be able to put me into a trance and undo my cycle of self-abuse in a single session. I knew that I needed to be de-programmed. However, when we spoke on the phone, she suggested I would be an ideal candidate for the Emotional Freedom Technique. So, I went in for an appointment. She listened to me tell her about my host of problems (real and imagined) and then we rated them in order of importance and severity. She had me tap on various points of my body. If I were an outsider observing the process, I probably would have thought it asinine, but, as an insider, I was aware that I was experiencing tremendous relief. In the first session, we dealt with years of accumulated anger towards my stepfather, rage I'd felt since childhood. With one EFT session, all of my anger simply evaporated. I felt forgiveness and peace. More importantly, I felt free.

Over the remaining weeks and months, I returned numerous times for EFT sessions, targeting everything from my behaviors to my emotions. EFT alone did not heal my eating disorder or free me completely from my emotional bondage. It did, however, free me from many of the issues that came to light. I believe that this failure stemmed from working on a cognitive level rather than a physical one. I got to the emotions that needed unblocking through talking about my issues then tapping them out. The reason EFT worked with my anger towards my stepfather was that I could clearly identify the series of experiences that made me hurt and angry and unblock my stuck negative energy through tapping. EFT failed to work with my bulimia not because of any deficiency in the technique, but because of my inability to diagnose the root cause of my disease.

Because the origins of my eating disorder made no intellectual sense to me, I could not achieve a sense of awareness of the causes or conditions through my intellect. I was asking the wrong questions, and so was every mental health professional and medical specialist I sought out, including my EFT practitioner. The problem was that they were asking my brain "What is the emotion that drives your bulimia and where does this feeling come from?" It was only when I began questioning my body, through yoga, that the real answer could emerge and I could use EFT to tap out my fear and heal fully and completely.

I need to be clear about the impact of EFT: EFT works! It heals the energetic imbalances that cause our negative emotions, and it is a rapid and effective technique. I believe that the **only** limitation of EFT, as it is currently used, has to do with diagnosing the cause of the energetic imbalance. We must invite the body to diagnose and treat itself.

It is essential, then, to identify "the issue" if you hope to be free of it. My experience as a practitioner has taught me that, when using EFT alone, pinpointing the issue cognitively can be problematic. The lives of the eighteen clients described in this book and the circumstances that led them to seek EYE illuminate the inevitable self-ignorance that can occur in the mind's eye. The case histories of these eighteen clients as they presented and the approach of conventional EFT elucidate the value of EFT while simultaneously revealing the shortcomings of using this technique on its own. Their experiences reveal the types of issues that can be self-diagnosed from a more cognitive standpoint. That said, EFT is an essential component of EYE. It is imperative that you learn EFT in order to fully resolve your emotional pain and reset your body's energy. Without the additional tool of yoga, EFT often lacks full efficacy. However, enough about the shortcomings of EFT. As far as I am concerned, the technique is only limited when we utilize a brain-based method of diagnosis. Once we employ the body as its own diagnostician, through EYE, the practical application of the technique becomes much more effective. We can then heal.

Holly, Lisa, and Tim

Holly's EFT Experience:

Having been in conventional talk-therapy for years, Holly had not cognitively processed, or resolved, the many issues that emerged during the course of her Emotional Yoga Experience. She couldn't, as these issues came to light during our physical explorations of her feelings. When she first sat opposite me, she expressed being overwhelmed by her borderline personality disorder.

Holly sought EYE because she craved relief from the symptoms of her disorder: impulsivity, emotional neediness, extreme emotional instability, and fear of abandonment. In the course of her experiences on the yoga mat, the underlying current of depression that surged beneath her emotional surface broke free. Through EFT alone, she would not have gotten through her internal unrest because she wasn't even aware it existed.

Despite her symptoms, Holly reported feeling generally okay. She could identify her behaviors, but not the underlying emotions. The only feeling she could isolate was fear.

"I don't feel sad or angry or anything," she told me. "I just feel like I'm broken. I can't control what I do or say. I can't stop acting out. I'm afraid all the time that I'll do or say something terrible."

Holly could see how her behavior was impacting her life, getting in the way of her ability to connect with others, ending her relationships and alienating people. But she couldn't change.

"I feel so disjointed when it comes to relationships," she told me honestly. "I do things on impulse and don't even think."

Had we employed EFT alone, no doubt Holly's identifiable issues would have improved. But, she would only have been able to go as deep as her mind could take her. Clearly, her mind was a perilous place to be. Holly's thoughts weren't entirely her own, as evidenced by the impulses propelling most of her actions. She had no control over her behavior, because her behavior had control over her. It was Holly's body, not her mind, that held her truths.

Equalize Your Energy

Impulsive Actions

Identify an impulsive behavior that creates problems in your life. Choose an action that you perform instinctively, without thinking of the inevitable consequences. Some examples might include binging, over-spending, reckless driving, shoplifting, yelling, destroying property, or being promiscuous. Tap out the issue using the setup phrase: "Even though I impulsively (state the action), I deeply and completely love and accept myself." Use the entire three-step EFT process: the Setup, the Sequence, and Repeat the Sequence. For best results, "tap out" the issue between two and four times.

Holly's Example: "Even though I impulsively (act out), I deeply and completely love and accept myself."

REMEMBER THE ENTIRE EFT SEQUENCE (**pages 34-35**):

1. KC, 2. H, 3. EB, 4. SE, 5. UE, 6. UN, 7. CH, 8. CB, 9. UA

Even if you are unaware of the forces driving your impulsive actions, EFT can and will change you. However, without going deeper, digging underneath your symptoms to excavate your underlying emotions, it is unlikely that you will be forever cured of your compulsive behavioral patterns. Still, you will likely experience a significant reduction in urges to act out and a lessening of the intensity that drives this behavior.

Lisa's EFT Experience:

Lisa was far too competent and collected to self-assess her childhood emotional wounds. She was dismissive of any approach that wasn't entirely intellectual.

"If I can just re-conceptualize how I see my life, I'm sure I can let go of my anxiety."

I tried not to smirk as I asked her what techniques she had already tried to change her thinking.

"CBT, MBCT, DBT, MBSR, ACT, NLP, ETT, EMDR, psychoanalysis, and hypnosis," Lisa rattled off a list of initials and methods quickly.

"Did they help?" I asked her.

She paused, contemplatively, and shrugged, "I guess. Temporarily. A little. Clearly, I must not be doing them right."

Lisa couldn't quite wrap her mind around the fact that her intellect could not rescue her from her emotions.

She described her issues as entirely oriented in the present. She said she experienced feelings of anxiety and insecurity, and, although they were minor, she was seeking relief from them.

"I feel like I don't matter, like despite how hard I try, I'll always be invisible," she confessed. "I just can't believe that anything I have to say matters. I feel like no one cares about me. Even I don't care about me."

Lisa described the incongruity between her actions and her emotions: "No one could ever guess how insecure I really am. I just want my feelings to match my actions."

She knew she had self-esteem issues, but cognitive interventions could not access her deeper emotional underpinnings. Lisa's insecurities were not brain-based, but were energetic wounds suffered in childhood. Lisa required the experience of reentering her history physically. She literally needed Child's Pose to transport her back to her youth. There she could re-experience the sensations of voicelessness and vulnerability that had persisted into adulthood.

Equalize Your Energy

Childhood Issues

Identify an experience from childhood that bothered you. Ideally, select one that still troubles you now. Even if you feel that you've let go of the event, select an incident that was deeply upsetting to you at the time. Some examples might include the birth of a sibling, your parent's divorce, getting a bad grade on a test, or being bullied. Tap out the issue using the setup phrase: "Even though, when I was a child, <u>(state the experience)</u>, I deeply and completely love and accept myself." Use the entire three-step EFT process: the Setup, the Sequence, and Repeat the Sequence. For best results, "tap out" the issue between two and four times.

> **Lisa's Example: "Even though, when I was a child, (<u>I once heard my mom say she didn't want me</u>), I deeply and completely love and accept myself."**

REMEMBER THE ENTIRE EFT SEQUENCE (**pages 34-35**):

1. KC, 2. H, 3. EB, 4. SE, 5. UE, 6. UN, 7. CH, 8. CB, 9. UA

Cognitively, Lisa would never have been able to articulate her experiences because her belief in self-sufficiency blinded her to her unexpressed emotional neediness. What emerged during her EYE session was a deep-seated wound stemming from having been ignored and neglected as a child. As a highly competent, highly intelligent woman, Lisa mentally dismissed her childhood experiences. She either minimized them or told herself that she had outgrown their impact. She is the type of client who typically stalls in EFT, experiencing rapid relief in certain areas only to find herself still stunted in others with no apparent explanation. Lisa was like I was when I first sought EFT and was able to let go of my rage, but not my bulimia.

Tim's EFT Experience:

In Tim's case, EFT alone would not have allowed him to go deep enough behind his mask to identify and release his pain. He couldn't talk about his secret until his body gave him permission to feel how deeply denying his sexual orientation was hurting him.

Tim told me that talking about his sexuality was something that he never allowed himself to do. Even after his attempted suicide, Tim had not divulged his sexual preference to his therapist. Instead, he had blamed all of his emotional problems on superficial concerns and avoided revealing the lie underlying his unhappiness. Despite what he told himself and others, Tim had never been, and would never be, heterosexual.

Tim's self-loathing was intense and all-pervasive. He lived his life so far in the closet that there would have been no "coming out" without his body at the steering wheel of his healing journey. Tim was not able to talk about his sexual orientation openly because his mind was closed to all possibility of his sexual self-expression. It was only after he felt the discomfort of forcing himself into straight angles in a physical context (in yoga's Triangle Pose) that he could embrace and reorient himself, both on the mat and in his life.

Equalize Your Energy

Identifying the Lie

Answer the question: "What lie do I tell myself or others?" After you have identified the lie that you are living with, you can use EFT to release the disconnect between the truth that your body holds and the lie that exists in your mind. Some examples of possible lies include having an affair, cheating on a test, stealing, being deceitful, fudging the truth about your age or weight, or saying that you feel a certain way about a situation when you don't. It doesn't matter if the lie is outright or an issue of misrepresentation. Isolate it. Tap out the untruth using the setup phrase: "Even though I lie and tell myself/tell others that <u>(state the lie)</u>, I deeply and completely love and accept myself." Use the entire three-step EFT process: the Setup, the Sequence, and Repeat the Sequence. For best results, "tap out" the issue between two and four times.

Tim's Example: "Even though I lie and tell myself (<u>it doesn't matter that my family doesn't know I'm gay</u>), I deeply and completly love and accept myself."

REMEMBER THE ENTIRE EFT SEQUENCE (pages 34-35):

1. KC, 2. H, 3. EB, 4. SE, 5. UE, 6. UN, 7. CH, 8. CB, 9. UA

As long as we lie to ourselves, self-delusion limits the effectiveness of EFT, and we cannot become the people we were meant to be. Living a lie is something that many of us do. Over time, the falsehoods that we tell ourselves and others become so deeply entrenched within us that the truth eludes us entirely. This internalization of untruths is part of why cognitive and verbal modalities often miss the mark.

For instance, I have several clients who have children that told me, emphatically, before their EYE sessions, that parenting was the greatest thing in their life and their very reason for living. However, during their EYE sessions, their bodies told a story of unmet expectations and feelings of emptiness. On the mat, these clients confessed to being miserable, depressed, and disconnected, admitting that their lives felt emptied by parenthood rather than enriched by it. Paradoxically, in going within, feeling the true emotions that lay beyond the scope of their intellects, they could heal these emotional disconnects and actually come to feel that which they earnestly hoped to feel. These same parents, following EYE recalibration, spoke of surges of genuine love that had not existed before.

One young mother informed me, surprise showing in her eyes, "I love my son in a way that I never imagined possible. Before, I *knew* that I loved him, but now I *feel* that love. It's like the love came out of my head and went into my heart."

Vanessa, Jennifer, and Kristin

Vanessa's EFT Experience:

Two years of talk-therapy had done little to alleviate Vanessa's perpetual grief. When she first came to see me for her EYE session, she said, "I'm feeling sad and I'm not exactly sure why. I should have moved past it by now."

Vanessa was so used to minimizing her emotional response to her miscarriage that her words denied the truth even though her body spoke volumes.

Vanessa was able to trace her sadness back to her miscarriage, yet no amount of therapy or positive thinking had helped her to escape her grief. EFT, used on its own, probably would have helped her to achieve a degree of healing by balancing her body's energy, but it may not have freed her from her debilitating depression. Of course, Vanessa certainly could have "tapped out" those feelings. She was capable of identifying her sadness, grief, and loss. However, the deeper, physically-held negative emotions were inaccessible through thinking about them alone.

Examining Vanessa's self-diagnosis from an EFT-perspective, it is clear that, even prior to coming to see me, she had identified significant components of her emotional struggle. If I had worked with her strictly as an EFT practitioner, I would, no doubt, have teased out a number of useful setup phrases: "Even though I have this <u>sadness about not having children,</u> I deeply and completely love and accept myself." "Even though I <u>had a miscarriage two years ago</u>, I deeply and completely love and accept myself." "Even though I have <u>this depression</u>, I deeply and completely love and accept myself." "Even though I have <u>not moved past it</u>, I deeply and completely love and accept myself."

Any of these setups would have worked to effectively alleviate some of Vanessa's pain. However, her body's visceral sense of loss went deeper. For Vanessa, part of her had died when Laurel died. Until we delved deep with yoga, she lacked the ability to access the profound sense of emptiness her body had been feeling ever since her miscarriage.

Vanessa knew her pain stemmed from losing her baby, but identifying the physical sensation of emptiness, which she did with yoga, provided the springboard for her Emotional Yoga Experience. Without the additional tool of yoga, EFT probably would have lacked full efficacy and may not have been enough to fully heal Vanessa's wounds.

Equalize Your Energy

Grief and Loss

Identify a loss that you are grieving. We have all experienced losses, whether real or imagined, seemingly insignificant or monumental. Some examples might include the death of a loved one, a breakup, the loss of a job, or even the loss of your favorite sweater. Tap out the issue using the setup phrase: "Even though I lost my <u>(state the loss)</u>, I deeply and completely love and accept myself." Use the entire three-step EFT process: the Setup, the Sequence, and Repeat the Sequence. For best results, "tap out" the issue between two and four times.

Vanessa's Example: "Even though I lost my (<u>baby</u>), I deeply and completely love and accept myself."

REMEMBER THE ENTIRE EFT SEQUENCE (pages 34-35):

1. KC, 2. H, 3. EB, 4. SE, 5. UE, 6. UN, 7. CH, 8. CB, 9. UA

When dealing with loss, it is important to note that our bodies experience actual and perceived losses in the same way. We can miss that which we once had or that which we imagined we had or that which we hoped to one day possess. Remember high school? You had that unrequited crush…When he or she turned you down, didn't it feel soul-deflating? You never actually had a relationship to lose, yet the perceived loss felt just as crushing as when, later on, you broke up with your first boyfriend or girlfriend. This just goes to further illustrate the fact that events are not responsible for our feelings. Our bodies' energetic responses to events are what cause us to feel devastated (even in the wake of non-experiences).

EFT heals the energetic imbalances that cause our negative emotions, and it is rapid and effective. We must invite the body to both diagnose and treat itself. While EFT alone will not completely illuminate the darkness of your internal room, it will shine enough light to reveal the path before you, to help you to see the utility of recalibrating your body's energy system to positively impact your emotions. I invite you to use EFT to release some of the grief that you can already identify cognitively in your own life. As you employ the technique, you will no doubt discover an improvement in your energy level and moods.

Jennifer's EFT Experience:

Jennifer was a vision of perfection, but, upon deeper inspection, she didn't seem alive. She seemed robotic.

Jennifer's OCD was clearly destroying her life. Her worst enemy – her mind – created mental loopholes she couldn't break out of. Jennifer described her counting and checking rituals as "more essential than breathing." She couldn't imagine a life without her obsessive thoughts and compulsive actions. OCD alienated her from others. It had even forced her husband to move out, a separation born of desperation and her inability to let go of her inflexibility. For Jennifer, a physical approach to healing offered what her mind could not – relief.

"I want to focus on fixing my marriage. When I'm in OCD-mode, I'd rather fixate on washing my hands or cleaning the house than on the important things. The reason my husband moved out was because I missed going to our last therapy session together. I was folding laundry and couldn't leave the house until I was finished. The more I tried to rush, the more mistakes I made. He kept calling from the therapist's office, but I couldn't leave the house. It's pathetic."

Jennifer's relationships suffered and the circumference of her life was so small as to be claustrophobic. Yet, change eluded her.

Equalize Your Energy

Obsessive Thoughts

Identify an obsessive thought that repeatedly causes you trouble. This may be an actual obsession of the type that OCD sufferers experience or it may be negative self-talk, worry, your to-do list, or an endless loop of memories. Some examples might include thinking about a mistake you made, worrying about how you look, counting compulsively, or fixating on a specific problem and not being able to let go of it. Tap out the issue using the setup phrase: "Even though I am obsessing about (state the issue), I can let go and live in the moment." Use the entire three-step EFT process: the Setup, the Sequence, and Repeat the Sequence. For best results, "tap out" the issue between two and four times.

Jennifer's Example: "Even though I am obsessing about (numbers and counting), I can let go and live in the moment."

REMEMBER THE ENTIRE EFT SEQUENCE (pages 34-35):

1. KC, 2. H, 3. EB, 4. SE, 5. UE, 6. UN, 7. CH, 8. CB, 9. UA

Jennifer had suffered from OCD for as long as she could remember. She couldn't identify the source of her obsessions; however, she could feel them getting progressively worse. She felt completely out of control. She was unraveling, constantly trapped within her thoughts. The nonverbal modality of EYE transported Jennifer from her mind into her body, bringing her out of the problem and into the solution. Granted, EFT alone would have helped her to eliminate some of her specific, identifiable obsessive thoughts and compulsive actions. However, EYE dug up the weeds of Jennifer's OCD from their roots, enabling her to entirely eliminate her obsessions and compulsions. She became flexible and free, as connected as she had once been controlled.

Kristin's EFT Experience:

Kristin's anorexia ate away at her, destroying her physically and emotionally. Her severe body dysmorphia prevented Kristin from being able to see herself or her body clearly. She couldn't seem to conceptualize the degree to which her disease had taken over her life. At 87 pounds, Kristin consumed less than 400 calories a day and, yet, she reported that she felt fine. She said she never got hungry and couldn't understand why her loved ones worried about her.

"I'm not really that bad," she told me, lying to herself as much as to me. "I'm a naturally thin person. I know that, technically, I'm anorexic, but I do eat."

I am not sure if EFT, used by itself, would have helped Kristin let go of her eating disorder. My experience working with eating disordered clients indicates that reentry into the body is a critical healing component for those whose behavior is fueled by body hatred. Once she connected with her body, Kristin encountered her long-buried hunger. Her experiences exemplify the mind-body disconnect that often makes cognitively-based therapies ineffective. Using the mind to diagnose emotional issues is as ineffectual as starting a fire by rubbing two sticks together. It may eventually work, but more often than not, the process tends to only cause frustration. EYE is like a match that illuminates a pathway, Since the body offers an easy entry point towards wellness, yoga can act as an accelerant, igniting the flames of our inner healing fire.

Equalize Your Energy

Food and Feelings

Identify a food or food-related behavior that causes you to feel uncomfortable or that you use in order to alleviate discomfort. For example, you might feel guilty about your love affair with chocolate or you might crave potato chips every time that you experience stress. Maybe anytime you feel stressed, you start skipping meals or lose your appetite altogether. Here, your setup phrase might take on one of two forms depending on if the emotion leads you to the food or food-related behavior or if the food itself generates feelings within you. Tap out the issue constructing your setup phrases as follows: "Even though I eat (state the food) to deal with (state the feeling), I deeply and completely love and accept myself" or "Even though eating (state the food) makes me feel (state the feeling), I deeply and completely love and accept myself." Tap out the food/feeling connection using the entire three-step EFT process: the Setup, the Sequence, and Repeat the Sequence. For best results, "tap out" the issue between two and four times.

Kristin's Example: "Even though eating (anything) makes me feel (out of control), I deeply and completely love and accept myself."

REMEMBER THE ENTIRE EFT SEQUENCE (pages 34-35):

1. KC, 2. H, 3. EB, 4. SE, 5. UE, 6. UN, 7. CH, 8. CB, 9. UA

From my own healing experiences, as well as my work with clients, I have come to believe that all of us develop certain detrimental connections between food and our feelings. Sometimes, this can manifest itself in severe eating issues – episodic binging, starving, purging, crash dieting, food obsession, or emotional eating. Other times, these issues may be more subtle – like associating eating certain foods with "being bad," following the latest diet fads, or using food as a reward. Or, maybe, you have certain food sensitivities, allergies, or intolerances. EYE can help with all such issues and liberate you to develop a healthy relationship with food. Once you release your negative energy around eating, you will see food as fuel and will be able to feed your body according to its needs.

Morgan, Lori, and Maureen

Morgan's EFT Experience:

Morgan couldn't remember being raped. Because of her alcohol consumption, Morgan had mental "blank spots."

"They did it," she told me. "They even bragged about it afterward. At school, they called me the 'sorority slut.' Who knows? Maybe, I did want it, but I don't have memories of any of it."

Ashamed and embarrassed, she continued to attend parties and to get drunk as her male classmates continued to take advantage of her. Because Morgan repeatedly put herself in dangerous situations, even after the first rape happened, she dismissed her experiences, thereby minimizing her pain.

She came to me seeking relief from her alcoholism. Yet, she drank because she didn't want to remember being brutalized. Terrified that, if she stopped drinking, her suppressed memories would rise to the surface like detritus floating to the top of a pond, she kept drinking to oblivion and cutting herself to avoid feeling anything other than numb. Even if her brain forgot, her body remembered. Her body required healing, so, on this physical level, we began.

Equalize Your Energy

Willful Forgetting

Identify an unpleasant event that you would rather not remember. Maybe, this is something that you blocked out. You may not have any recollection of this incident – the mind may have successfully relegated this memory to the background. It may be something that you were told happened, but can't recall. Or it may be an event that haunts your every waking moment. Any painful memory that you have either forgotten or would like to forget will suffice. Some examples might include getting dropped off for your first day of kindergarten and crying uncontrollably, being molested, or breaking your arm at age four. Tap out the issue using the setup phrase: "Even though I don't want to remember (state the experience), it happened, and I deeply and completely love and accept myself anyway." Use the entire three-step EFT process: the Setup, the Sequence, and Repeat the Sequence. For best results, "tap out" the issue between two and four times.

Morgan's Example: "Even though I don't want to remember (men having sex with me while I was passed out, drunk), I deeply and completely love and accept myself."

REMEMBER THE ENTIRE EFT SEQUENCE (pages 34-35):

1. KC, 2. H, 3. EB, 4. SE, 5. UE, 6. UN, 7. CH, 8. CB, 9. UA

If, like Morgan, you are petrified that remembering your past will dredge up painful emotions, hurting you all over again, you can relax. While some techniques do carry with them the inherent danger of re-traumatization, EFT is virtually pain-free. In order for the technique to be effective, you do not have to dive headfirst into your emotional pool. With EFT, you can dip a toe into the waters of your past, checking the temperature without diving too deep and risking drowning. You will have to think about the problem, but you won't need to hyper-focus on the past. With EYE, the mind can get out of the way entirely and your body can articulate its experiences. You may never have to bring your cognitive awareness back to your past at all. Your body may completely circumvent the mental minefield that you are afraid will explode within you if you revisit your past.

Morgan's desire to mentally block out her memories of being violated stripped her of her ability to cognitively, or verbally, access her experiences. Instead, in order to heal, she needed a way to circumvent her mind and allow her body to speak for her. I should note as well that Morgan was a self-mutilator, her arms and legs marred by long, jagged scars. Her brutal, violent relationship with her body made it especially important for her to give her body a voice to tell its story through yogic inner-inquiry.

Lori's EFT Experience:

Lori sought relief from anxiety and back pain. The twenty-nine-year-old felt a constant fervor propelling her toward action. Even sitting in a chair before our EYE session, as she took off her shoes, she multitasked: untying the laces of her left shoe, bouncing her right leg restlessly, biting her bottom lip, fidgeting, talking nonstop, and chewing absently on a piece of gum, all at the same time.

"Sorry I'm moving so much," she acknowledged, "but I'm always moving. It's even worse when I'm nervous."

Had we done EFT without incorporating EYE, Lori would not have had to tune in to her body's whispers. As long as we remained in a constant state of motion, she could drown out her emotions. Always moving, always running, always thinking, Lori's Emotional Yoga Experience forced her to be still and acknowledge the emotion beneath her motion. Had we done EFT without EYE, Lori would not have had to tune into what her body was trying to tell her.

Equalize Your Energy

Distraction

Identify one of the ways in which you distract yourself from your emotions. These distraction methods may involve actions or thoughts. Select anything that you use in order to disconnect from yourself. Some examples include eating, watching TV, focusing on mundane problems, searching the Internet, or doing busywork. Tap out the issue using the setup phrase: "Even though I use (state the behavior) to distract myself from my feelings, I deeply and completely love and accept myself." Use the entire three-step EFT process: the Setup, the Sequence, and Repeat the Sequence. For best results, "tap out" the issue between two and four times.

> **Lori's Example: "Even though I use (constant movement) to distract myself from my feelings, I deeply and completely love and accept myself."**

REMEMBER THE ENTIRE EFT SEQUENCE (pages 34-35):

1. KC, 2. H, 3. EB, 4. SE, 5. UE, 6. UN, 7. CH, 8. CB, 9. UA

Distraction is not necessarily a "bad" thing, but when you find yourself using diversion to escape from your obligations, EFT can break through whatever barriers exist between you and your goals. Distraction can also keep you from living a life that truly reflects your desires.

Have you ever heard the saying "procrastination is perfectionism in disguise"? Think about how many times you have avoided taking the next step in some area of your life because you feared that you wouldn't get it "right," because of low self-esteem or because your brain convinced you to ignore the fact that every fiber of your being was urging you to live differently. I know, firsthand, how it feels to live incongruously – with your body and soul craving more than your brain will allow you to seek. When I worked in finance, I wanted to quit, but my brain wouldn't give me permission to obey my body. I urge you to do what I did. Stop hiding from, or suppressing, your negative feelings. Instead, start identifying and releasing them. Stop procrastinating and start tapping!

Maureen's EFT Experience:

Maureen originally thought that the source of her anxiety was work-related.

"I'm good at my job, but I doubt myself and my decisions," she told me. "It doesn't matter how many promotions I get or compliments I receive, I always feel like I'm about to be fired."

Maureen operated in a perpetual state of panic. She was convinced that, no matter how hard she tried, she would never measure up to her coworkers. Maureen was a workaholic, checking emails constantly.

She was glued to her Blackberry. In fact, she brought it with her to her first EYE session.

"Do you mind if I keep this on vibrate in case work calls?" she asked me. Even though our first session took place on a Saturday, she still felt she had to be in touch with work. "It could be important."

According to Maureen, if she could just relax about her job, her life would be perfect. Yet, as she discovered during her Emotional Yoga Experience, her anxiety was not caused by work. Instead, Maureen's feelings of inadequacy were rooted in abandonment issues that dated back to her childhood. As an adopted child, Maureen had felt unloved and unworthy even though, cognitively, she knew that people loved her. She had to internalize self-acceptance rather than intellectualize it.

Equalize Your Energy

Anxiety

Identify a situation in your everyday life that makes you feel anxious. Some examples might include work, dating, social situations, or public speaking. Tap out the issue using the setup phrase: "Even though I have this anxiety about (state the situation), I deeply and completely love and accept myself." Use the entire three-step EFT process: the Setup, the Sequence, and Repeat the Sequence. For best results, "tap out" the issue between two and four times.

Maureen's Example: "Even though I have this anxiety about (work), I deeply and completely love and accept myself."

REMEMBER THE ENTIRE EFT SEQUENCE (pages 34-35):

1. KC, 2. H, 3. EB, 4. SE, 5. UE, 6. UN, 7. CH, 8. CB, 9. UA

Even though Maureen's anxiety expressed itself at work, it was not about work. A typical EFT therapy session might have required her to "tap out" her fear of getting fired, her endless need to achieve, or her obsessive focus on her career. Yet, underlying all of the anxiety was a deeper feeling of rejection. Here was an abandoned child whose biological parents had given her up. No matter how much Maureen grew up or how much perspective she gained, her core energetic disruption needed to be corrected before she would ever be able to recognize her own worth.

Mrs. Walker, Ruth, and C.C.

Mrs. Walker's EFT Experience:

Mrs. Walker raged at everyone within earshot. Her primary problems were immediately evident to all of us. She was angry and she had cancer.

"What the hell do you want?" she growled at the poor nurse unlucky enough to be on dinner duty.

"I brought you your meatloaf and mashed potatoes," said the nurse, a friendly, overweight, young woman, smiled shyly at her.

Mrs. Walker glowered at the food and then back at the woman, "I haven't eaten that crap since I first got here. This damn food will kill me faster than the cancer. My daughter is bringing me something in a little while. Why don't you eat it? You fat girls will eat anything."

The nurse wordlessly set the dinner tray on the table. Her bottom lip began to quiver as she blinked back tears.

"What?" the old woman sneered meanly at me.

"Maybe we should do some EFT," I suggested.

With Mrs. Walker, I began by employing EFT alone. Since she was resistant to doing any of the "New Age crap" that comprises my life's work, I didn't want to introduce a body-based modality right away. Even so, EFT alone helped her tremendously. In fact, it possibly even created a physical environment wherein healing could occur and her cancer therapy could begin to work. Cancer is the body eating away at itself, so

I maintain that employing EYE's body-focused approach to healing, after first laying the groundwork with EFT, was tremendously beneficial. Yet, it is impossible to say what EFT, used by itself, would have done without the later inclusion of yoga. In Mrs. Walker's case, I added EYE to accelerate her healing process, but even used by itself, EFT had a tremendous and immediate positive impact. EYE fully eradicated Mrs. Walker's issues; however, EFT alone may have been enough. As a point of clarification, I do not claim that EFT or EYE had the power to to cure cancer. I simply maintain that, at least in Mrs. Walker's case, they helped remove any energetic and emotional barriers to healing and paved the way toward potential remission.

Equalize Your Energy

Anger

Identify a person or a situation that makes you angry. You can choose a recent event or one from your past, someone who is still a part of your life, or someone with whom you no longer interact. Some examples might include your boss, your spouse, a sibling, a co-worker, a friend, not getting something you felt entitled to, an unfair set of circumstances, or even being cut off in traffic. Tap out the issue using the setup phrase: "Even though I am angry at/about (state the person or situation), ***I deeply and completely love and accept myself." Use the entire three-step EFT process: the Setup, the Sequence, and Repeat the Sequence. For best results, "tap out" the issue between two and four times.***

Mrs. Walker's Example: "Even though I am angry at (my husband for dying), I deeply and completely love and accept myself."

REMEMBER THE ENTIRE EFT SEQUENCE (pages 34-35):

1. KC, 2. H, 3. EB, 4. SE, 5. UE, 6. UN, 7. CH, 8. CB, 9. UA

I should note that, after a few EFT sessions, Mrs. Walker became a markedly different woman, smiling kindly and saying "please" and "thank you." A few weeks after beginning EFT, I arrived at the hospital to see Mrs. Walker and found her sitting with the poor, plump nurse that she had reduced to tears during the meatloaf exchange. They were sitting together, tapping on themselves.

"I'm teaching Marsha to do EFT," Mrs. Walker told me proudly. "She wants to lose 20 pounds and I'm going to help her."

Later, Marsha told me that the entire staff was grateful for the transformations that they were witnessing taking place in Mrs. Walker.

"She even apologized to me," Marsha said. "If EFT can change her from a mean old bitch into a kind, generous person, I'm sure that it can help me to lose 20 pounds."

My EFT Experience:

When I was a teenager, I was raped by my drug-addicted boyfriend. To hide my shame and my low self-esteem, I lied about it. I lied to myself so often and so convincingly that I persuaded myself that the event never happened. However, I lived with the impact of the incident: I couldn't trust men; I couldn't achieve orgasm; I was sexually stuck. My inability to develop intimate relationships was self-evident. The reasons, however, eluded me. I was stuck and I was unable to figure out why.

In my case, my brain was like a vault. It had locked away all of my memories of my ex's cruelty. I sometimes awoke from nightmares, soaked in sweat, and I occasionally had images flash on my mental screen – me screaming while he lay on top of me, the stale odor of pot smoke, the taste of blood as I bit my lip while struggling beneath him. Foggy images and intermittent nightmares aside, I wasn't aware of my past; so, of course, there was no way I could express it or examine it. Not cognitively, anyway. My body articulated its pain in every shudder, every dissociative moment, every time I recoiled at a man's loving touch.

Yoga offered me entry into my past so I could see what my body was trying to show me, what I refused to acknowledge: I was raped. My mind had no answers. My body contained the harsh truth, and, once I entered it with yoga, EFT became effective. I let go of the experience and then let go of my sexual dysfunction.

Equalize Your Energy

Intimacy Issues

Identify one barrier that gets in the way of your ability to create intimate connections, either with yourself or with others. Some examples include a history of dysfunctional relationships, sexual abuse, feeling distant from others, or dishonesty. Tap out the issue using the setup phrase: "Even though I have trouble with intimacy because of (state the issue), I deeply and completely love and accept myself." Use the entire three-step EFT process: the Setup, the Sequence, and Repeat the Sequence. For best results, "tap out" the issue between two and four times.

> **My Example: "Even though I have trouble with intimacy because (I was raped), I deeply and completely love and accept myself."**

REMEMBER THE ENTIRE EFT SEQUENCE (pages 34-35):

1. KC, 2. H, 3. EB, 4. SE, 5. UE, 6. UN, 7. CH, 8. CB, 9. UA

The word intimacy, or into-me-see, involves the ability to be transparent either with ourselves or with another person. This process of stripping back the barriers to being seen allows us to fully connect with ourselves and others. And, while deeply rewarding, the very notion of building intimacy can be terrifying. Looking within and acknowledging the truth contained within our bodies is a critical first step in building self into-me-see. Our brains often prevent us from seeing within, which is why EFT can be too brain-based a technique for increasing our capacity for connection, when what is needed is a sensory diagnosis.

Ruth's EFT Experience:

Ruth came to EYE because she was experiencing shoulder and back pain.

"I'm fifty-three and I feel like I'm eighty," she told me. "I've tried everything, but nothing helps. My chiropractor suggested this, but I'm not all that optimistic. I mean, how is the Emotional Yoga Experience going to help me? My problems are physical."

As it turned out, these "physical problems" had unseen emotional causes and, once Ruth was able to release life's pressures, her body moved more freely, and her pain vanished. For her, it took the inward-looking modality of yoga to acknowledge her dissatisfaction at work. However, EFT, used on its own, is often extremely effective in reducing or eliminating physical pain. Because our minds allow us to identify the sources of our pain and pinpoint the physical symptoms (if we have a headache, a backache, or premenstral cramps, we know it), EFT can quickly and easily eradicate these symptoms.

Equalize Your Energy

Physical Pain

Identify one physical complaint that you are suffering from. This can be anything from chronic back pain to constipation to diabetes. Choose an issue that appears to have a physical cause without regard to possible contributing emotional factors. Some examples might include backaches, muscle soreness, a pinched nerve, headaches, menstrual cramps, or dental pain. Tap out the issue using the setup phrase: "Even though I have this (state the physical issue), I deeply and completely love and accept myself." Use the entire three-step EFT process: the Setup, the Sequence, and Repeat the Sequence. For best results, "tap out" the issue between two and four times.

Ruth's Example: "Even though I have this (pain between my shoulder blades), I deeply and completely love and accept myself."

REMEMBER THE ENTIRE EFT SEQUENCE (pages 34-35:

1. KC, 2. H, 3. EB, 4. SE, 5. UE, 6. UN, 7. CH, 8. CB, 9. UA

Remember, physical pain can generate emotional suffering and, conversely, emotional pain can manifest itself as physical suffering. Did you ever notice that your back spasmed right before your college reunion, that your neck refused to move on the day of your daughter's wedding, or that your menstrual cramps became debilitating during an important meeting at work? People with "bad backs" have a tendency to throw them out during times of stress. Sufferers of fibromyalgia (a debilitating chronic pain syndrome) often become depressed due to their body's unrelenting achiness. I am not saying all pain is psychosomatic; rather, I'm suggesting our bodies are directly connected to our emotions. No matter which arises first, the physical or the emotional pain, EFT can provide relief on one or both levels.

C.C.'s EFT Experience:

One of the most effective applications of EFT is in treating physical issues – such as pain, indigestion, headaches, or even constipation. This is because physical issues are often readily diagnosed and identified by both our bodies and our minds. When she first came to see me, one such constipated client (we'll call her "C.C.") hadn't had a bowel movement in ten days. Believe me, she knew exactly how long it had been since she had last gone and was fully able to diagnose her problem. What C.C. remained unaware of, however, were the ingrained emotional experiences that contributed to her physical discomfort.

From my experiences as an EFT practitioner, I can guess that, working solely with this method, C.C. likely would have felt relief almost immediately but would probably have had the problem reoccur at a later date. Until she could identify the emotional unrest within and unblock herself from that, her bowels were doomed to retain waste just as her psyche could not digest toxic emotional residue.

"I've seen EFT before," C.C. informed me blithely. "And, frankly, it strikes me as...well..." she seemed to be searching for a fitting description, "It seems like bullshit. I mean, how is tapping on my body going to make me take a crap?"

I smiled at her. I could have explained energy meridians and the science behind EFT, but, instead, I suggested that we do some tapping and see what happened.

"Even though I can't let go of all of this old shit, I deeply and completely accept myself," C.C. tapped and said. "Even though I haven't taken a poop in ten days and my body feels gross, I love and accept myself anyway." She rolled her eyes in disbelief that EFT could help her.

I told her to keep tapping. It wasn't long before her body began emitting loud, gurgling noises.

In C.C.'s case, she knew she needed help letting go of "crap." EFT alone likely would have been entirely effective, although yoga's twisting poses stimulated her digestion and elimination and so speeded her process. For C.C., the physical results were immediate. In fact, she needed to use the bathroom forty-five minutes into her EYE session.

However, EYE brought a benefit which she had not expected – emotional relief. If she had only performed EFT on the issue of her constipation, C.C. could not have let go of the emotional "crap" that was clogging her life with the same deleterious results as the bile in her bowels.

Equalize Your Energy

Feeling Stuck

Identify one area in your life in which you feel stuck. Some examples might include hitting a weight-loss plateau, entering into the same types of dysfunctional relationships over and over again, stalling out on a

creative project, feeling stuck in a job, or being unable to make a change in your life. Tap out the issue using the setup phrase: "Even though I feel stuck because I (state the issue), I deeply and completely love and accept myself." Use the entire three-step EFT process: the Setup, the Sequence, and Repeat the Sequence. For best results, "tap out" the issue between two and four times.

C.C.'s Example: "Even though I feel stuck because (I can't poop), I deeply and completely love and accept myself."

REMEMBER THE ENTIRE EFT SEQUENCE (pages 34-35):

1. KC, 2. H, 3. EB, 4. SE, 5. UE, 6. UN, 7. CH, 8. CB, 9. UA

Tia, Brooke, and Lester

Tia's EFT Experience:

An incest survivor, Tia found herself trapped, again and again, within a cycle of destructive male-female relationships. Every interaction that she had with men was clouded by her history of abuse. Her ability to see these issues would have made her a good candidate for EFT intervention, yet I doubt that she would have allowed herself to arrive at the painful truth, which EYE revealed.

"I was sexually abused as a child. I've worked through a lot of my pain and shame in therapy, but I keep ending up in abusive relationships anyway. I want freedom from my past, but I'm haunted by it."

The problems Tia was able to identify were her incestuous abuse, her patterns of dating men who treated her cruelly, her low self-esteem, her hyper-focus on her body, and her use of sex to get her needs met.

"My father abused me," she admitted. "I had a lot of rage. Now, I think I've forgiven him and myself. He hasn't been a part of my life since I was eleven."

Tia had been in therapy for years, but had never admitted, even to herself, that she had liked being sexualized by her father. Tia's cognitive filters got in the way of her ability to properly self-diagnose this fact. To acknowledge how much she had loved her father and how desperately she had wanted him to come to her bed at night was too much for Tia's rational, adult brain. EFT intervention likely would have felt inadequate because, until her body brought her deeper into the feelings beneath her shame, Tia would have only been able to chip away at the edges of her emotional iceberg.

Equalize Your Energy

Familial Dysfunction

Identify one familial relationship or event that disturbs you. Maybe, it is a person or an experience from your nuclear family, or maybe it's someone or something that deals with your extended family. Whether the issue concerns your current family or your family of origin, select a specific person or event. Some examples might include a distant father, an overbearing mother, adult children who shut you out of their lives, sibling rivalry, a particularly upsetting Christmas memory, a Thanksgiving debacle, or being left off of the guest list for your cousin's wedding. Tap out the issue using the setup phrase: "Even though it bothers me that, in my family, (state the specific source of your disturbance), I deeply and completely love and accept myself." Use the entire three-step EFT process: the Setup, the Sequence, and Repeat the Sequence. For best results, "tap out" the issue between two and four times.

REMEMBER THE ENTIRE EFT SEQUENCE (pages 34-35):

1. KC, 2. H, 3. EB, 4. SE, 5. UE, 6. UN, 7. CH, 8. CB, 9. UA

In Tia's case, based on her ability to self-diagnose her own issues, her years of therapy, and her existing self-awareness, some possible cognitively-based setup phrases would have been:

"Even though my father molested me, I deeply and completely love and accept myself." "Even though I choose emotionally unavailable men, I deeply and completely love and accept myself." "Even though I am ashamed that I was abused, I deeply and completely love and accept myself."

These setup phrases would have touched at the emotions surrounding Tia's core shame, but not at the true source-point of her dysfunction. Tia's desire for her father and the fact that she enjoyed it when he touched her was the root of her shame. That root lay so deep beneath her emotional earth that her brain lacked the power to dig it up. Only her body could excavate that specific layer of Tia's shame. Only EYE could free her entirely from the prison of her pain. However, in the absence of total freedom, EFT would have been like a parole officer, letting her out, but keeping her on a tight leash.

Brooke's EFT Experience:

Since her rape, Brooke had been unable to leave her house and was unwilling to face her life or the world. No amount of cognitive or behavioral therapy helped. She had dissociated from her body and could not verbally articulate what was occurring around her socially or emotionally.

EFT, used on its own, could have helped alleviate some of Brooke's symptoms. It might have allowed her to let go of some of her memories. However, this technique alone would not have offered the rapid positive results that the Emotional Yoga Experience achieved. Overall, EFT has been extremely useful in treating PTSD, so I am not discounting its effectiveness. However, in Brooke's case, EFT would have offered little relief because she was so profoundly disconnected from herself and her emotions. EYE, on the other hand, rapidly diagnosed the core issue while bringing Brooke back into her body in a way that EFT alone would not have been able to achieve.

Brooke's mind entrapped her. It was where she fled after her body was so terribly violated. She couldn't get out of the prison of her mind without EYE. The brutality of her rape had impacted Brooke's body so profoundly that only a body-based approach to healing could have restored her to physical and emotional wholeness. We had to get Brooke's mind out of the way. Not only was it not facilitating a solution, despite all the therapy she had tried, but Brooke was petrified to let go of her fear because her mind told her that, as soon as she became confident again, she would become the target for more violence.

"If I never go out, I can never get hurt," she told me. "I don't know if I want to get better. I want to want to get better. I feel bad for my mom. She should have her own life, but, instead, she has me acting like I'm a five year old."

In any cognitively-based therapy, Brooke's fear of getting well was in itself a major impediment to healing. She was afraid to let go of her fear.

Equalize Your Energy

Primary Problem

Identify the one issue that you would consider to be your "primary problem." Likely, it is the complaint that brings you into therapy again and again or the issue which prompted you to buy this book. Some examples include: depression, anxiety, PTSD, OCD, excess weight, addiction, or chronic pain. Tap out the issue using the setup phrase: "Even though I have this (state the problem), I deeply and completely love and accept myself." Use the entire three-step EFT process: the Setup, the Sequence, and Repeat the Sequence. For best results, "tap out" the issue between two and four times.

Brooke's Example: "Even though I have this (<u>Post-Traumatic Stress Disorder</u>), I deeply and completely love and accept myself."

REMEMBER THE ENTIRE EFT SEQUENCE (pages 34-35):

1. KC, 2. H, 3. EB, 4. SE, 5. UE, 6. UN, 7. CH, 8. CB, 9. UA

Brooke's chief complaint was her intense fear of venturing outside of her house alone. She knew that this terror paralyzed her, making it impossible for her to function in the world. Moreover, she could identify her trauma as the source of her agoraphobia. However, so many layers existed underneath the surface of the issue. Brooke dissociated during every cognitively-based therapeutic intervention. At these times, she became incapable of talking about her fears. If we had stuck to EFT methodology, Brooke would never have been able to focus on her primary problem or to tap it out. She would have done what she did during every other cognitively-based intervention. She would have shut down.

Instead, Tree Pose brought Brooke into the fear that lay underneath her agoraphobia. With yoga, Brooke felt the internal physical tremors occurring within her body, on a cellular level. Her inability to balance physically clearly mirrored her inability to achieve emotional stability. It was from this place of physical instability that Brooke was able to perform EFT on her fear. She regained energetic equilibrium and, almost immediately, her body and her life became more balanced. A cognitive approach would never have broken through Brooke's mental barriers to healing; however, EYE circumvented her brain and disentangled the snarls of negative emotions contained within her body.

Lester's EFT Experience:

Lester came to his EYE session willing only to look at his anxiety issues.

"Sometimes, it feels like a heart attack. I be getting these panic attacks all the time," he told me, averting his vacant, bloodshot eyes from my gaze.

Lester claimed that his only real problem was anxiety – overwhelming and intolerable anxiety. Yet, in the course of his session, he revealed a fifteen-year long cocaine addiction. Deep-seated fears drove his habitual stimulant usage. His anxiety led him to use drugs and using them created more anxiety in him. Lester told me that he had originally had no intention of telling me about his cocaine addiction.

"I ain't never told no one," he shook his head at me, as if still unable to believe the extent of his confession.

This self-sacrificing and overburdened family man was not one to risk opening up about his emotions. Taught to be proud and independent, Lester could never have admitted to his addictions without yoga providing a door into his emotions. In his family, it had been unacceptable for Lester to admit weakness or to ask for help. For him, the physical act of yoga disarmed his mental resistance to admitting his drug addiction. Boat and Locust Poses put him in touch with his core, which enabled him to admit his real problem. As we joked later, yoga literally rocked his emotional boat.

Equalize Your Energy

Breaking Bad Habits

Identify a habit that you would like to let go of. This can include any behavior from drug or alcohol use to nail biting to cigarette smoking. Tap out the issue using the setup phrase: "Even though I can't stop <u>(state the habit)</u>, I deeply and completely love and accept myself." Use the entire three-step EFT process: the Setup, the Sequence, and Repeat the Sequence. For best results, "tap out" the issue between two and four times.

Lester's Example: "Even though I can't stop (using cocaine), I deeply and completely love and accept myself."

REMEMBER THE ENTIRE EFT SEQUENCE (pages 34-35):

1. KC, 2. H, 3. EB, 4. SE, 5. UE, 6. UN, 7. CH, 8. CB, 9. UA

EFT can be a tremendous tool for enabling us to move forward in our lives, and to let go of whatever habits are adversely impacting us. Many people have used EFT to successfully quit smoking, lose weight, stop watching TV, or to break any number of unhealthy habits.

As soon as Lester admitted that he was addicted to cocaine, EFT could help him; however, without yoga to disarm him and dispel his internal resistance, Lester never would have exposed his cocaine habit to me or to any other treatment provider.

Margaret, Samantha, and Beth

Margaret's EFT Experience:

Margaret couldn't possibly have identified her feelings without the benefit of yogic self-inquiry because she was completely disconnected from her emotions. An attractive woman with fair skin, a slim build, and delicate mannerisms, Margaret looked and sounded much like Eliza Doolittle after Henry Higgins had made her over in *My Fair Lady*. Proper, prim, and pretty, she presented herself as if she were the embodiment of the stereotypically reserved Brit, but beneath her seemingly impenetrable exterior, beneath the numbness she felt, Margaret's body contained an unreachable undercurrent of emotion. She told me she felt nothing, as if she were hollow inside.

"I'm empty. It's quite aggro. I want to feel something, but I can't."

Margaret's ex-husband had cheated on her, which led her to shut down emotionally. Her trust had been so deeply violated that she couldn't talk about her experiences without turning off her emotions entirely. On the phone, and even in person, before yoga opened her up to her true feelings, Margaret took a dismissive attitude towards her experiences.

"He was an arse, but I'm better off without him," she told me blithely. "I'm over all of that unpleasantness now."

Even though Margaret verbally expressed feeling resolved about her ex-husband's infidelities and the dissolution of her marriage, her body told a different story entirely.

Equalize Your Energy

Betrayed Trust

Identify a time when your trust was violated and identify the person who broke your trust. From an objective standpoint, this violation may appear to be major or minor. However, it should feel significant to you. Some examples might include being lied to by a friend, being cheated on, having money stolen from you, or even finding out that your parents lied about the existence of Santa Claus. Tap out the issue using the setup phrase: "Even though (identify the person) broke my trust when he/she (state the action), I deeply and completely love and accept myself." Use the entire three-step EFT process: the Setup, the Sequence, and Repeat the Sequence. For best results, "tap out" the issue between two and four times.

Margaret's Example: "Even though (my ex-husband) broke my trust when he (repeatedly cheated on me), I deeply and completely love and accept myself."

REMEMBER THE ENTIRE EFT SEQUENCE (pages 34-35):

1. KC, 2. H, 3. EB, 4. SE, 5. UE, 6. UN, 7. CH, 8. CB, 9. UA

After trust has been broken, it is easy to shut down in order to resist becoming vulnerable again. Sometimes, after a person has been betrayed, he or she stops being open in an effort not to reveal too much or to feel too exposed. This may even manifest itself in a reluctance to expose one's innermost feelings to a therapist or other mental health professional. Once trust has been violated, the mind may instruct a person to withhold information, choosing not to divulge their most sacred truths.

Margaret was wounded. She trusted no one to hold her confidences because she believed that, if her ex-husband could violate her (which he did habitually and repeatedly over the course of their marriage), then no one was worthy of her trust. Including me. Including her.

Until Margaret allowed her body to articulate her pain, she could not face the extent of her violation or its lasting impact on her. EFT would have only skimmed the surface of the issue, not because of any defect in the technique, but because diagnosing a loss of trust as the main problem might have been impossible.

Margaret was adamant that her problem was feeling disconnected and numb and that she had moved past "that old malarkey." As it turned out, her ex-husband's infidelities remained a constant source of pain until she could release her feelings of betrayal from her body, just as she had released them from her mental awareness.

Samantha's EFT Experience:

Clearly, Samantha's layers of physical fat were a sign that her body was holding onto emotional pain.

In self-diagnosing the issues beneath excess weight, Samantha guessed at the problem: "Maybe I'm using food to punish myself. Maybe I'm sabotaging my own happiness. Maybe I use food to deal with my emotions. Maybe it's just a bad habit. I don't know. My parents were both overweight. Maybe it's nature and nurture."

She wrinkled her forehead, perplexed by her own self-destructive cycle. Unwrapping a piece of gum with long, languid motions, Samantha put it into her mouth and began to chew. Her dark, purplish-red lips smiled at me despite her obvious unhappiness. Samantha described her relationship with food as perilous, threatening, and unsafe. She spoke of eating to the point of pain.

Yet, when she looked to her body, rather than her mind, to answer the question,"What do you want food to do for you?" her immediate response was, "Keep me safe."

Samantha ate to feel insulated against her emotions. Her feeling of being unsafe in a hostile world drove her to use each compulsive bite to create emotional insulation, giving her a false sense of security in an insecure world. No wonder she couldn't stop binging! Letting go of her protector (food) would have exposed her to pain. Since Samantha was unable to submerge herself in the emotional waters that were drowning her dieting resolve, she was doomed to sink every time she tried to swim out of her fat. Mentally, Samantha hated everything about her relationship with food and described her eating habits as abusive and dangerous, but her body's nonverbal experience of eating belied Samantha's words. Cognitive therapy and behavioral modification failed, again and again, because food was her refuge.

EFT might have helped her to reduce her consumption and thereby increase her willpower around food, but it would not have required the sensory bodily awareness that her Emotional Yoga Experience involved. EFT, used by itself, would not have allowed Samantha to reestablish a sense of internal safety or to completely let go of her false reliance on food.

Equalize Your Energy

Establishing Safety

Identify an area in your life where you feel, or have felt, unsafe. Maybe it is a relationship. Maybe it is a situation. Some examples include having felt threatened as a child when your parents argued, feeling at risk when driving, feeling insecure in your marriage, or feeling unsafe in your own skin due to a medical condidtion or a history of abuse. Tap out the issue using the setup phrase: "Even though I feel unsafe

because (identify the situation), I deeply and completely love and accept myself." Use the entire three-step EFT process: the Setup, the Sequence, and Repeat the Sequence. For best results, "tap out" the issue between two and four times.

> **Samantha's Example: "Even though I feel unsafe because (I can't stop eating compulsively), I deeply and completely love and accept myself."**

REMEMBER THE ENTIRE EFT SEQUENCE (pages 34-35):

1. KC, 2. H, 3. EB, 4. SE, 5. UE, 6. UN, 7. CH, 8. CB, 9. UA

The body is complex and wise; yet, it is also primitive. It has urges, impulses, and instincts that drive it. It does not have the ability to interpret its own feedback. For example, imagine that you are walking in a dark alley alone at night. You hear footsteps and turn around to see a figure emerge from the shadows. A surge of fear immediately arises within you. The shadowy form brandishes a weapon. You begin to panic. Your heart rate speeds up. Your pulse races. A surge of adrenaline floods your body.

Never mind that, upon closer inspection, the figure belongs to a seventy-year-old grandmother and the "weapon" in her hand is a cane, which she is using to help her hobble along. Knowing this cognitively won't help you to immediately relax. Your body has already experienced a shock and it will take a while for it to return to a state of normalcy. As this example demonstrates, our bodies feel first. We interpret the body's messages later on. Our physical selves hold feelings in ways that we cannot always express or identify.

For Samantha, the urge towards self-protection was intense. Food activated her feeling of safety. She was never able to identify the origin of this food/feeling connection; however, it didn't matter for her letting-go process. Seventy-five pounds effortlessly melted off of her. Who knows why Samantha viewed the world as a shadowy, menacing place? Who knows why she fervently ate as a way to fight or flee the impending doom that never really existed? Who cares?

EYE turned the light of her emotions on, freeing her to see clearly. Just as, in the illumination of the streetlamp, it became clear what had petrified you was a harmless old woman and no real danger existed, EYE revealed to Samantha that whatever danger she had perceived did not exist. Food had become her jailer rather than her rescuer. It turns out that she is safer now than she ever was – safe from heart disease, diabetes, and the other potential consequences of obesity.

Beth's EFT Experience:

Logic defied Beth's emotions. She knew, intellectually, that she'd been a good mother, but, emotionally, she had trouble letting go of her self-doubt. Beth believed that she hadn't measured up as a parent.

"I was a bad mother," she told me. "Well, I wasn't the worst mother, but my daughter once told me she hated me. Everyone tells me all kids say things like that to their parents at some point, but I'm sure they're just being nice."

I looked at Beth.

She wore a delicate silver bracelet on her slender wrist. The shiny metal trinket was engraved with the words, "We love you, always and forever."

Beth had just finished telling me, after I had complimented her on her gorgeous bracelet, that her daughter and her granddaughter had given it to her as a gift.

"It wasn't for a special occasion," she had said. "They just gave it to me because they thought I might like it."

Now, Beth looked down at the bracelet, too. She looked guiltily at me, as if she'd been caught in a lie.

"I know what you're thinking," Beth said. "Maybe, they do love me. I don't know. They say they do, but I'm convinced they hate me. I know I failed them both."

Then, clearly tortured by the discrepancy between the evidence and her emotions, Beth began to cry. No matter how much positive self-talk she fed herself or how often her daughter and granddaughter told her that they loved her, Beth felt inadequate. She couldn't get herself to believe what she knew to be true: her daughter loved her. Beth's body was the bridge connecting her thoughts to her feelings. It was the missing link in the chain of her healing.

Equalize Your Energy

Wounding Words

Identify a time when someone said something that hurt you deeply. Try to recall their wounding words as precisely as possible. Some examples include your fourth-grade classmate saying "You have cooties," your boss calling your work "subpar," your parents referring to your sister as "the pretty one" and you as "the smart one," or your ex telling you "I've fallen out of love with you." Tap out the issue using the setup phrase: "Even though (identify person) told me that (words that they said), I deeply and completely love and accept myself." Use the entire three-step EFT process: the Setup, the Sequence, and Repeat the Sequence. For best results, "tap out" the issue between two and four times.

Beth's Example: "Even though (my daughter) told me that (she hated me), I deeply and completely love and accept myself."

REMEMBER THE ENTIRE EFT SEQUENCE (pages 34-35):

1. KC, 2. H, 3. EB, 4. SE, 5. UE, 6. UN, 7. CH, 8. CB, 9. UA

Intelligence and emotional stability have absolutely no correlation. I know. I was a brilliant bulimic with a 4.0 GPA and my head, literally, in the toilet. I have met geniuses who were suicidally depressed. We're all familiar with the paradigm of the "tortured artist." Stop trying to think yourself well. Allow yourself to experience your emotions, then recalibrate your energy, turning negative feelings into positive ones.

Bringing Balance: Putting it Together, Using EFT to Equalize Your Energy

Holly, Lisa, Tim, Vanessa, Jennifer, Kristin, Morgan, Lori, Maureen, Mrs. Walker, Ruth, C.C., Tia, Brooke, Lester, Margaret, Samantha, and Beth all suffered from internal unrest. Their brains couldn't be trusted to diagnose the disruptions in their bodies. Each of these clients was limited in their ability to self-diagnose their issues. As such, their healing experiences clearly reveal the inherent limitations of self-assessment.

EFT is an intensely verbal, rational discipline developed by an engineer. EYE, on the other hand, is a nonverbal, body-oriented, experiential approach that often defies logic. Drawing upon the foundations of yogic self-inquiry, EYE trusts the body. Although EFT is an energetic approach to recalibrating the body's energy system, I have found that it sometimes misses the mark. The genius behind the Emotional Yoga Experience is that it operates entirely at the level of the body, both diagnosing and treating emotional issues physically.

Armed with the EFT technique, and after having been exposed to the stories of these clients, I hope that you have emerged with two truths: EFT powerfully restores the body's energy and EFT is limited in terms of diagnosis. Using this technique, on its own, without the benefit of yoga, you can rebalance your body's energy system. EFT will shine enough light to reveal the path before you, helping you to see the value of recalibrating your energy. However, EFT alone may not completely illuminate the darkness of your internal room. It can, however, positively impact your emotions.

I hope that this chapter has shown you (maybe, for the first time) that your mind is limited in diagnosing and treating your emotional issues. If you have been blind to the need for this non-traditional, but incredibly effective, approach for healing, I hope that you will now enthusiastically apply EFT to your easily-identifiable issues. When you do, you will surely experience a positive energy surge and feel better and freer. Keep in mind, though, that, as you do the EFT exercises, you will also likely experience firsthand the limitations of EFT when used independently, without yoga.

EFT eliminates repetitive emotional patterns quickly and effectively. I advocate performing the technique with some degree of regularity because everyday life can often be energetically upsetting to our bodies. We are over stimulated. We experience stressful situations. We are human beings who have already lived through many emotionally draining situations and who are in need of energetic replacement. One week, or even one day, of practicing EFT may be enough to free you permanently from many of your old patterns of behaving and thinking; however, your body has stored years of energetic traumas and disruptions. EFT works most effectively on those problems that you can identify and on those issues that arise within your mental landscape. You have to first be aware of the emotions, the thoughts, and the behaviors before EFT can help you to help yourself. I find that, if you diligently practice the EFT techniques, you will transcend many of the limiting belief systems that afflict you.

Based on my personal healing, client experiences, and research into the energy of our emotions, I created the following chart as a useful tool for practicing EFT. Use it as an experiential and diagnostic guide. Take the time to identify the issues that you are already aware of, and then release them.

Use EFT to Release Negative Energy

Emotion:	Situation:	Setup Phrase:
Anger	Identify a person you are angry at or a situation that you are angry about.	"Even though I am angry at (person or situation), I deeply and completely love and accept myself."
Sadness	Identify an event or a situation that makes you sad.	"Even though I am sad about (event or situation), I deeply and completely love and accept myself."
Grief	Identify a loss that you are grieving.	"Even though I am grieving the loss of (person, place, or thing), I deeply and completely love and accept myself."
Fear	Identify a person or a situation that you are afraid of. Note: If you have a phobia, begin there.	"Even though I am afraid of (person or situation), I deeply and completely love and accept myself."
Guilt	Identify an action from your past that you feel guilty about.	"Even though I feel guilty about (action), I deeply and completely love and accept myself."
Jealousy	Identify someone in your life (now or in the past) of whom you are/were jealous.	"Even though I am/was jealous of (person), I deeply and completely love and accept myself."
Self-Pity	Identify a current or past situation that makes you pity yourself.	"Even though I feel self-pity when I think about (situation), I deeply and completely love and accept myself."
Frustration	Identify something in your life that you are frustrated about.	"Even though I am frustrated because of (situation), I deeply and completely love and accept myself."

Emotion:	Situation:	Setup Phrase:
Shame	Identify something about yourself or your life that you feel ashamed of.	"Even though I am ashamed of myself for (issue), I deeply and completely love and accept myself."
Regret	Identify an action that you took in the past that you now regret.	"Even though I regret the fact that I (action), I deeply and completely love and accept myself."
Worry	Identify a potential situation or experience in your life that causes you to worry.	"Even though I worry about (possible or inevitable situation), I deeply and completely love and accept myself."
Stress	Identify the issue in your life that currently causes you the most stress.	"Even though I feel stressed about (issue), I deeply and completely love and accept myself."

The Emotional Freedom Technique (EFT) is a critical component of the Emotional Yoga Experience (EYE). It is incredibly effective in its own right, yet EFT's reliance on a cognitive diagnosis limits the technique's usefulness. As the second component of EYE, EFT is an essential piece in your energy-balancing work. However, this technique alone is not enough to bring about the radical transformations that this book describes. On the other hand, the Emotional Yoga Experience offers a visionary approach to healing by combining yoga and EFT. If you are eager to move ahead to a system of self-healing that both diagnoses and treats emotional issues on a physical level, please read on.

Emerge: Use EYE to Free Yourself from the Prison of Your Pain

The Emotional Yoga Experience (EYE) circumvents the mind and, instead, focuses its attention on the body. The technique is most effective when we allow our body's answers to come out spontaneously, rather than waiting for our minds to interpret its messages. It is only by engaging our emotions physically, feeling the unrest within, and interrogating our bodies that we can discover those aspects of ourselves that need healing and which are unreachable through our minds.

Our bodies retain negative emotions like water-logged sponges. Yoga brings awareness to these emotions and EFT wrings them out, releasing those old held onto feelings. Yoga helps with emotional awareness and release occurs once EFT positively impacts the body's energy, because EYE both diagnoses and treats emotional issues at a physical level. Relief is felt as this approach changes us from the inside out.

When a client first comes to see me for an individual Emotional Yoga Experience session, I ask them what physical or emotional pain has brought them to me. Yes, I am particularly concerned with what happens on the mat and not overly concerned with what they share with me. Yes, the mental notes I make are from a practitioner's viewpoint, but I view myself as an interrogator of the body. I begin by digging into absorbed emotional angst and excavating stored pain. I question their bodies. Rather than focusing on their self-diagnosed issues, during this first session we might concentrate on a wide variety of emotions like joy, trust, fear, surprise, sadness, disgust, anger, and anticipation, offering a general check-up with subsequent sessions possibly dealing with a single emotion stored in a single (or in multiple) body part(s). Or, if one issue surfaces, we might delve immediately into that.

I should mention that the Emotional Yoga Experience offers an elastic, intuitive approach to healing. Because of this, I often change my treatment approach, focusing on a particular emotion or on specific parts of the body in cases where a single traumatic event, a debilitating emotional problem, or a physical ailment is present. In those cases, I use EYE to immediately douse whatever physical or emotional flames are sweeping through a person like wildfire, destroying any hope of peace or tranquility. I focus on putting out the fire before assessing the damages or cleaning up the debris.

In most cases, however, my initial goal is to unblock as much stored negative energy as possible, releasing those major impediments to joyful living that arise within the body. I have learned it's best to do a generalized clearing out in order to truly and accurately assess a client's present emotional state and kick-start the healing process. Because of the inherent mental interference that we all experience, when trying to accurately assess our emotional experiences, it is often difficult for people to correctly diagnose their own emotional issues.

If the cause of all negative emotions is a disruption in the body's energy system, then the body is our best resource for both diagnosing and healing these energetic imbalances. Using yoga to identify the stored pain and shame within the body, then using EFT to release whatever emotions are uncovered, it is possible to non-verbally access and release emotions to achieve full healing.

You've seen how yoga offers emotional awareness and EFT offers a pathway out of pain. The following section will demonstrate how combining yoga and EFT radically transformed each client's life. See the entire EYE process, beginning on the next page, to better understand EYE in action.

Holly, Lisa, and Tim

Holly's Emotional Yoga Experience:

As wild as her hair, so too were Holly's impulses and actions. Holly was as miserable as she was beautiful. At thirty two years old, she had ruined relationships by cheating on men whom she loved deeply and had twice ended engagements.

"I don't know why I ruin everything," Holly told me. "I hate myself. I hate being a borderline. I just want to be normal."

As Holly transitioned into Warrior II Pose, her arms stretching out from her shoulders like two lightning rods – fierce and strong – I asked her, "In what ways does your borderline personality disorder act as armor, keeping you protected?"

"I hurt others before they can hurt me," Holly said.

We tapped out the destructiveness that led her to injure others. With each new yogic revelation, Holly shed layers of self-hate and blocked energy.

In Downward Dog, Holly came face-to-face with her own depression and her past suicide attempts. Emotions welled up from within – rage and shame and pain. Her body brought her into her urge to destroy herself. Confronted with the harsh reality of her stored depression, Holly tapped it out and tapped out the specific memories of each of her three suicide attempts. She had "processed" her pain, but she had not released it. She finally let it go on the mat, not from her mind but from her body.

After Holly's EYE session, her life changed dramatically. Following our work together, many of her symptoms disappeared entirely. EYE opened her up to be kinder to herself and to others. Seeing the transformation in her, Holly's psychiatrist recommended that she lower the dosages of her medications. This allowed Holly to feel her true emotions more fully and to experience a deeper sense of connection with herself and with the world. She still hasn't met "the one," but she has improved her relationships with friends and family members and with herself. Holly told me she doesn't sabotage herself these days.

Lisa's Emotional Yoga Experience:

Clad in a sweater and loose-fitting linen pants, Lisa was the picture of corporate casual. Her red hair framed her face in a shapely bob. She looked like a slightly fleshier version of Miranda from *Sex in the City*, and, much like her television doppelganger, Lisa was a long-time devotee of therapy.

"I need to deal with my issues," she said. "The more I think about my life, the more I realize how my perceived inferiority and low self-esteem have impacted everything."

Lisa was highly skeptical about EYE.

"I know yoga has demonstrated health benefits," she conceded. "But the energy component of EYE strikes me as…" she searched for the right word, and finding none said, "I imagine that there may be a placebo effect, but your claim that EYE can resolve emotional problems can't possibly be accurate."

I made a deal with Lisa on the spot: she agreed to check her intellect at the door and see what happened and I agreed that, if she didn't feel internal shifts by the end of the session, I would refund her money. Much of Lisa's pain was preverbal. She couldn't access it cognitively. Her body held her sorrow, and it was only by exploring its stored pain through yoga that she could begin to connect with the long-buried source of her angst. In Child's Pose, she wept copiously as her body transported her back to feeling ignored as a child.

Her mother's indifference had hurt. Together, we explored the stored sadness that the woman had carried with her from infancy. For as long as she could remember, Lisa had felt small and invisible.

In Wide Angle Forward Fold, with her legs spread and her torso folding forward, I asked Lisa how she kept herself small. Lisa shuddered with the dawning awareness born of yoga.

"I wanted to be a dancer. I dreamed of taking classes when I was younger. I loved hip hop, jazz, ballet, and tango. But I never did. Now, I won't ever dance unless I'm alone. I don't want anyone to see me dance."

In Dancer's Pose, Lisa felt a tightness in her chest at the recognition that she had always held herself back, making herself insignificant so as not to be obtrusive. However, as she tapped, Lisa began to let go of her valuation of her mother's opinions of her. For the first time in her life, Lisa recognized her own worth.

Since that session, Lisa has begun voicing her opinions, obtained a better job, and learned to set boundaries with her mother. She has even started taking Zumba classes at a local gym! Needless to say, she did not ask for her money back.

Tim's Emotional Yoga Experience:

Tim strode confidently into his EYE session and flashed a bright, toothy grin at me. As he greeted me with a handshake and a wink, he seemed to exude self-assurance. On the yoga mat, however, his body told the true story.

It was as if yoga were holding up a mirror, reflecting back a version of Tim that he never let anyone see. In front of me sat a man who hated himself. A gay man in his mid-forties, Tim was suicidally depressed. In fact, he'd previously attempted suicide.

"I'm a failure even at killing myself," he said, his voice thick with sadness.

Tim had spent most of his life cultivating the imaginary persona of a happy, clean cut, all-American man. With yoga, he let the walls down.

I had Tim transition into Bridge Pose, focusing on where in his life he felt like he was lacking in connection. He told me that he felt disconnected from himself and from others. We began tapping on these feelings.

As Tim sat in Staff Pose, I noticed that his spine tended to collapse into his body, as if he were lacking a backbone. The body often articulates our experiences for us. When asked where he felt like he lacked a backbone, Tim's eyes implored me like a lost and lonely puppy.

He slumped further into himself. "I'm gay," he confessed, "I can't tell my family and it's killing me. I've had a few serious boyfriends over the years, but they all left me eventually when I refused to come out of the closet."

In Corpse Pose, the disparity between the external persona that Tim projected (a confident, virile, heterosexual bachelor) and the internal identity that he was hiding from the world (an insecure, lonely, self-hating homosexual) became clear. We tapped out Tim's shame around his sexuality as well as his fear of owning his sexual orientation, especially with his family.

He left our session feeling enthusiastic and motivated to embrace life. In Tim's case, the evolution from self-deception to authenticity took several sessions as he released layers of energetic blockages and reconnected his internal circuitry. In subsequent sessions, more feelings came out on the mat. Tim's disavowal of his homosexual identity and his need to prove himself to his father tortured him. We tapped out the perceived weakness which was behind so much of his pain. We peeled back layers of emotional baggage.

In Goddess Pose, Tim said he felt hyper-aware of his pelvis, extremely exposed and incredibly lonely. He also said that there was something comfortable and reassuring about the posture.

"It feels right, but it's all wrong," he told me.

"And how does your experience in Goddess Pose feel like your experiences in life?" I knew the answer even before I asked the question.

Tim smiled, breaking out of his depression and realizing that, only in owning his feelings of being different, could he ever hope to feel comfortable.

Since then, Tim has become a more integrated person. He doesn't divulge his sexual orientation to everyone, but he has come out to his family and close friends. He is exploring the world now as an openly gay man rather than as a closeted one. In fact, Tim called me recently to tell me that he had met a man he really likes.

"I'm not sure if it'll work out or not, but for the first time in my life, I feel like I have a chance to be myself and to be happy. My mom actually invited both of us to the house for dinner this weekend."

Vanessa, Jennifer, and Kristin

Vanessa's Emotional Yoga Experience:

At thirty seven years old, Vanessa was experiencing an identity crisis. Throughout her twenties and early thirties, she had envisioned herself becoming a stay-at-home mom and building a "traditional" family.

It was through yoga that Vanessa connected with the sensation of emptiness that pervaded her – physically and emotionally. When her body began to tell its story on the mat, her pain became clear. Many women miscarry and, while disappointed, are not debilitated by their losses. They move on. Vanessa's miscarriage itself was not the issue; rather, of greater significance was the energetic impact of the event on her. Her body perceived the loss of her unborn child as a complete and total obliteration of herself. Her empty womb became an allegory for the emptiness that Vanessa experienced in every area of her life.

Vanessa came to me seeking a way to cope. Instead, she found a way to live.

In Happy Baby Pose, Vanessa fully felt her internal emptiness as she connected with the physical chasm within. The immense loss and longing that she had experienced on a constant basis since her miscarriage wasn't something that she could think her way out of. Physically, her energy had been short-circuited and whatever light had once illuminated her had been extinguished. She felt dead inside.

"I loved Laurel," Vanessa told me. "She was a part of me."

Together, Vanessa and I dove deep into the emotional undercurrents of her pain as her tears flowed. I took her through several rounds of tapping.

As she entered into Pigeon Pose, Vanessa was overcome by waves of the shame that she had been holding within her hips.

"It's my fault," she lamented, her torso draped over her leg in Pigeon Pose. "There's something wrong with me."

Together, we tapped out her self-recrimination.

However, it wasn't enough to let go of grief and shame or to come to terms with her life after having felt as if a part of her had died. Vanessa still needed to reawaken to life.

Vanessa hadn't felt true soul-enervating joy since her pregnancy two years before. Seeking to reinvigorate her and to restore a sense of purpose to her life, I instructed Vanessa to engage in invigorating breath work. While focusing on her body's inability to experience pleasure, I had Vanessa synch movement with breath in a series of gestures and breathing-patterns referred to in yoga as "Breath of Joy."

After performing this exercise, Vanessa realized that her biggest obstacle to feeling joy was not having had children. She viewed motherhood as part of her life's purpose and she and her husband had always shared a strong desire to have children. She lacked a sense of meaning and purpose and felt as if life itself was pointless. We tapped more. Almost immediately, Vanessa was reawakened to hope and began to feel a renewed sense of purpose. Interestingly enough, after her experiences on the mat, Vanessa decided to give motherhood another try.

Actually, to hear her tell it, she started "going with the flow."

Apparently, the flow worked. Eight months ago, Vanessa gave birth to a healthy baby boy.

Jennifer's Emotional Yoga Experience:

Rarely do clients arrive at their precise appointment time. Usually, they are either a few minutes early or a few minutes late for their sessions. Jennifer rang my doorbell at exactly the appointed time.

On the yoga mat, I guided her through a series of gentle stretches. Her inflexibility on the mat mirrored the rigidity that permeated every area of her life.

Jennifer explained that she was a slave to her rituals, locked within habitual patterns of counting, cleaning, checking, washing, grooming, and eating. Her Obsessive Compulsive Disorder was getting in the way of her living her life. It took her hours to get ready to go out. It took her close to an hour just to make breakfast in the morning. Jennifer was devastated because her OCD had robbed her of her life. In fact, she had separated from her husband as a result of her disorder.

"He can't live with my OCD," she told me.

Jennifer's OCD was especially limiting because of her ritualistic counting. Thirty-five years old, she had to do everything thirty-five times in order to feel safe. She switched the lights on and off thirty-five times each morning and thirty-five times each night. She even ate thirty-five cheerios for breakfast each morning with thirty-five raisins. She couldn't travel because of her rituals. She showered three times each day and washed herself according to the same methodological sequence every time.

She had been in therapy since the age of seventeen without ever having achieved relief from her OCD. Even after all her self-analysis, she couldn't pinpoint a specific cause of her OCD. She had developed the disorder as a child and Jennifer couldn't remember a time when her obsessions and compulsions hadn't dominated her life.

In Gate Pose, Jennifer flashed back to memories of her childhood home and the gated community where she grew up. She came from an extremely affluent family that had made accommodations around her obsessions and compulsions by modifying her life circumstances to allow her to function (at least partially). When Jennifer first met her husband at a family party (he was a friend of Jennifer's twin brother), she had seemed happy and flexible because she'd been able to operate within her own comfort zone. While her husband had always been aware that she was mildly neurotic and inflexible, he had no idea how all-consuming her OCDs were until after they were married and living together. Jennifer had believed that love and marriage would dispel her OCD. It hadn't worked.

In Mountain Pose, Jennifer felt the full-force of her emotional and behavioral rigidity. She felt stuck. EYE brought Jennifer into and out of the feelings driving her actions and obsessions. Her rigidly closed body unfolded during a series of yoga poses I deliberately chose with the aim of opening her physically and emotionally.

In Bow Pose, flooded with an upsurge of unidentifiable fear, Jennifer said, "It feels like I'll die if I stop counting."

Without ever identifying the source of her OCD, Jennifer pinpointed the sensation of panic that struck her whenever she felt out of control. Together, we tapped out this feeling. Paradoxically, Jennifer never discovered why she'd developed OCD – her formerly obsessive brain probably would have fixated on this fact – she simply let go of her rituals, rules, and routines.

Today, Jennifer showers once a day. She eats cheerios if and when she wants them. She is also free to eat eggs or oatmeal or whatever she happens to be in the mood for that day in whatever quantity she likes. She and her husband have reconciled and are organizing a trip to Italy. They are planning it together since Jennifer no longer needs to maintain complete control of every situation. And they're back in therapy, together, working on their marriage. Jennifer hasn't missed a single session.

Kristin's Emotional Yoga Experience:

Looking half-dead, Kristin walked into my office tentatively. Tall and rail-thin, the 87 pound stay-at-home mom had been struggling with anorexia for years. She had been spiraling downward at an alarming rate since the birth of her youngest child eleven months earlier. I've had a lot of success treating eating disordered clients and I have a special kind of empathy for this population because of my own bulimic history. Looking at Kristin, I willed myself not to cringe or to force-feed her a hamburger.

"You know why I'm here." Eyes downcast, Kristin didn't look at me as she scuffed the toe of her tennis shoe into the floor. "I don't want to go inpatient. I don't think I'm that bad."

However, all of her bony protuberances made the use of yoga props necessary. Pressing on her bones or lying on a hard floor would have been painful for Kristin. She had no physical insulation, so I fetched yoga props – bolsters, blankets, pillows, and blocks.

"I can't believe I'll need so much support and help," she told me as she sat down.

"How does needing support make you feel?" I queried.

"Inadequate," she said, looking away.

It was there that we began.

Kristin's harsh self-judgment was unremitting. She told me that she hated herself for not being able to take care of her own body.

"I'm a good mother to my three kids and a good wife to my husband. But, to myself, I am nothing. I don't want to be this person, this shell of a woman. My husband cringes whenever he touches me. We haven't had sex in months, and I can't even pick up my son."

Together, we tapped out her self-recrimination.

In Corpse Pose, Kristin looked deeper into herself and acknowledged her feelings of starvation. She was hungry – physically, mentally, and emotionally. After our session, as she was leaving, Kristin shook my hand.

"Thank you," she told me. "I think something may have changed."

"I'm sure it will," I smiled at her.

As she walked away, my heart bled for her. A week later, Kristin was back. Her palms pressing on the floor, her knees on a blanket, in Table Top Pose, I asked her what was missing from her own table.

"What won't you permit yourself to eat?"

Kristin started to cry. "I can't eat anything. My eating disorder won't let me."

She then began to list all of the foods and food-categories that were off-limits for her.

We tapped out her fears of eating each of these off-limits food items. Her list included meat, fish, cheese, sweets, fat, bread, rice, pasta, and many more. In the beginning, Kristin could only allow herself to eat fruit, fat-free yogurt, and vegetables.

In Supported Child's Pose, she began to cry. She told me that she didn't even know how to feed herself properly. Together, we tapped out her inability to meet her body's primal, basic hunger. Kristin had trouble verbalizing her issues or identifying the impediments to her feeding herself properly. We tapped anyway on what may well have been pre-verbal emotions dating back to infancy. A few weeks later, Kristin came into our next scheduled session smiling.

"I'm up to 92 pounds," she grinned. "It feels a lot easier to eat what my nutritionist wants me to."

Still, she was struggling with restricting liquids. After performing Supported Fish Pose, she told me that it felt as if liquids got stuck in her throat. She could barely swallow them.

"What does it feel like in your throat?"

"Like I'm choking."

"Have you ever choked before?" I asked her.

Suddenly, looking panic-stricken, Kristin began to cry. "I've never choked on anything," she told me. "But, when I was younger, my mom made all of us lunch. My sister was outside and I was starving, so I ate my lunch, then drank my sister's soda and ate her sandwich, too. She came inside and was so angry that she held me down and choked me. My mom had to pull her off of me. I was terrified."

The recollection of this long-buried incident had been stored in Kristin's body-memory for decades. It needed to be released through tapping.

Kristin strode confidently into her last session eating a bagel and finishing the last of her box of apple juice. Her eyes bright, her smile wide, she looked healthy and happy.

"I'm up to 130," she told me. Still, she reported struggling with intimacy issues.

Kristin had led a fairly sheltered life. In Lizard Pose, from the deep recesses of her stored physical memories, Kristin's body recalled her mother's voice telling her, "No boys will ever love and respect you if you let them just have sex with you. Having sex to have babies is one thing, but just doing it is wrong."

Even though Kristin had grown up, married, and given birth to three children, even though she had moved out of her mother's house and built her own life, and even though her mother had passed away several years earlier, Kristin had internalized the belief system at a level that went far beyond her consciousness.

"We're done having kids," she told me. "So I just feel wrong. I feel dirty."

We tapped out her reservations to physical intimacy and sexual satisfaction. Kristin let out a sigh of relief! She felt free. For the first time in as far back as she could remember, it was as if her body were truly her own.

Morgan, Lori, and Maureen

Morgan's Emotional Yoga Experience:

Some of the scratches on her forearms were old. Others had been made recently. Morgan used a razor to cut herself and her body offered a roadmap to her pain. Her eyes were vacant and her mouth formed a flat, expressionless line. Binge-drinking had made her bloated, red-faced, and about fifteen pounds north of pleasantly plump.

In Modified Pigeon Pose, I asked her what it was in her past that she was having trouble letting go of. Her hips opened the door to Morgan's memories and, together, we delved into the shame of her past.

"I hated being the 'sorority slut' or the 'drunken whore,'" she told me. "I don't even know what they did to me, but I hate myself for letting them do it."

Together, we tapped out Brooke's shame and self-blame. Instead of trying to access her feelings through mental awareness, we used her body to diagnose Morgan's emotional issues. Because she didn't have specific memories of her sexual exploitation, her vague recollections would have precluded traditional talk-therapy from being effective. With EYE, there were no barriers to accessing Brooke's stored pain.

"When I went to college. I went from being a person to being a plaything. No matter what happened in my life, before I left home, I felt like my parents would love me and forgive me and help me. Once I left, I felt like I was on my own."

After her first EYE session, Morgan stopped drinking and stayed stopped. She joined Alcoholics Anonymous and began to recover spiritually as well as emotionally. She decreased her cutting behaviors although she did not stop them immediately. Morgan told me that cutting felt like an essential part of her identity and it was only after she returned for a subsequent EYE session that Morgan could connect with her true core through poses that engaged her abdomen. Bridge Pose was incredibly illuminating for Morgan.

As she lifted her pelvis and felt her core engage, I asked her, "What is the missing link between your past, when you didn't hurt yourself, and your present?"

Morgan lowered her pelvis to the ground and hugged her knees fiercely into her chest.

"Self-respect," she told me. "I've lost all respect for myself. Because I don't value myself at all, it is so easy to abuse my body."

After we tapped out the barriers that got in the way of Morgan's ability to respect herself, she let go of cutting as an option. It's been several months since Morgan's last self-mutilation episode. She says that she occasionally has thoughts of cutting herself again, but that she cares too much about herself to give in to these transitory thoughts.

Lori's Emotional Yoga Experience:

A ball of energy, Lori was perpetually moving. A tiny woman, short and petite, she was at least a head shorter than I am and so slender that she looked as if an overly enthusiastic hug might break her in half. She strode purposefully through my door, then proceeded to pace back and forth, inspecting knick-knacks and rearranging items. Her overflow of nervous energy was contagious. Like sympathetic pregnancy or referred pain, Lori's restlessness radiated outward. I felt myself wanting to fidget. After corralling her onto her yoga mat, I invited Lori to sit still and focus on inhaling and exhaling. This seemed impossible to her.

"Breathing strikes me as a waste of time," she said without a trace of irony. "I mean, can't I do something while I breathe?"

She fidgeted constantly, peeling at the edges of her yoga mat with fingernails that she'd bitten down to the quick.

After about ten minutes of her frenzied activity, I asked her, "What would you feel if you stopped?"

"I don't know. I don't stop."

I had her sit in Easy Pose and breathe. Somewhere deep within her, the emotional dam broke.

"Life is so big and I'm so small," Lori cried. "It is so hard to be me. I want to jump out of my skin. Plus, with my back pain, I feel so trapped."

We tapped out her feeling of smallness and vulnerability. We also tapped out her physical complaint of back pain and her feelings of being trapped.

"If I stop moving, it feels like I'll die. I feel invisible and insignificant all the time."

I had her tap out these feelings.

The body is a mirror for our experiences. Lori told me that she hated being alone. She always needed to be surrounded by people or engaged in an activity in order to feel safe. Lori hated being by herself, especially if she wasn't doing anything. Even in sleep, she felt unsafe. The only way that Lori could sleep was if she drifted off while watching TV. She said that she needed the noise to distract her from her internal angst. We tapped out the pain that she felt at being alone.

In Crow Pose, Lori connected with how precarious her life had felt ever since her car accident. She had been stopped at a stop light when a drunk driver plowed into her from the side. It was no surprise that stopping, especially when alone, made Lori incredibly anxious. We tapped more.

I saw Lori four more times, for a total of five sessions. She is now completely free of back pain. What's more, she's taken up meditating and now does yoga twice a week at her gym. Incredibly, Lori no longer feels a need to move constantly. She has even stopped biting her fingernails, a habit that she'd had ever since childhood. Lori is comfortable in her own skin now.

"I may still be small," she told me. "But I no longer feel small."

Maureen's Emotional Yoga Experience:

Maureen's default emotional state was anxiety. Her inner-angst was especially prevalent at work. Despite her recent promotion and frequent accolades, she was convinced that she was about to be fired at any moment. On the outside, she appeared to be an extremely confident, capable, professional, self-possessed career woman. Internally, she never felt like enough.

In Warrior I Pose, Maureen felt defenseless, without protection against a world that terrified her. Together, we tapped out her feelings of vulnerability and isolation. In Standing Split, the pain of knowing that her biological parents had not wanted her hit Maureen full-force. Suddenly, she knew without a doubt that her feelings of not measuring up stemmed from her experiences of being abandoned as an infant. Maureen's constant vigilance and hyper-awareness and her fear that she could either be accepted or rejected for no discernible reason were born out of an emotional wound, which she suffered at birth. Until EYE, Maureen had never before identified this experience as the root of her fear. We zeroed in on her feelings of abandonment and tapped specifically on her experience of having been adopted.

No amount of talk-therapy could have convinced Maureen to internalize the self-love that her adoptive parents had poured into her, lovingly watering the garden of her mental and emotional development. She was incapable of allowing self-acceptance in until she let go of her stored negative energy around the issue.

A year later, Maureen's sense of self was completely different. She exuded an authentic air of calm self-assuredness. After EYE restored Maureen's self-confidence, she realized that she wasn't abandoned due to her own inadequacies, but that her parents must have been ill-equipped to raise her. She told me that, a few months after our first session, she had done some research on her birth parents. She got information about their lives and located them. She had even discovered that she had a half-sister who was divorced and living in Milwaukee. The last I heard, Maureen hadn't yet decided if she wanted to contact her parents or her sister. However, she felt a sense of empowerment after knowing more about the people who had given her up. Maureen told me that she felt closer to her husband and children than ever before. She even turned off her Blackberry at her daughter's dance recitals or when going to the movies with her son.

"I guess that I was abandoning my own family and my own life by focusing all of my energy on work," she admitted. "I don't do that anymore."

Mrs. Walker, Ruth, and C.C.

Mrs. Walker's Emotional Yoga Experience:

A word about pathological and physiological diseases: I am not a physician. Nor was Gray Craig (the founder of EFT) or Patanjali (the first known compiler of yoga philosophy). I do not believe that EYE is a cure-all. For instance, if a client were to come to see me with a dislocated shoulder or a bleeding wound, I would send him or her to the nearest emergency room for medical treatment. Allopathic and homeopathic cures work wonders and both Eastern and Western medicines have their place in healing the physical body. Still, EYE can facilitate the healing process by removing any emotional or energetic barriers to wellness.

For example, Mrs. Walker was withering away before her loved ones' eyes. Her family called me in to help her to make emotional peace as her body made the physical transition from living to dead. In her case, there was no pressure and no expectation that she would improve.

As Mrs. Walker's son-in-law told me when I arrived to see her, "We're not expecting much. My wife is about to have a nervous breakdown. I mean, she loves her mom, but if she didn't have to love her, she'd hate her. You've never met a meaner woman in your life."

During her first two sessions, Mrs. Walker barely talked except to complain about her daughter (whom she affectionately referred to as "that ungrateful cow") and to say that I was an idiot for sitting around tapping on my body like a monkey and murmuring to myself. Still, I practiced surrogate EYE, tapping on my own body, tuning into my own physicality as I noticed her body's physical cues. Although the topic of surrogate EYE extends beyond the scope of this book, I will briefly mention it here. One of the astounding elements of energy work is that it can be done on behalf of another person without needing to tap directly on their body. During Mrs. Walker's first two sessions, I tapped on my own body while she spoke. I said the affirmations for her. As I tapped on behalf of this crotchety old woman who was completely resistant to the idea of having me tap on her, my body became the portal for her healing experiences.

On my third visit to see Mrs. Walker, I was surprised when she greeted me by saying, "I don't know what you're doing, but I think your New Age crap is working. My doctors said my white blood cells have gone up some. Why don't you teach me to do your silly monkey crap?"

We practiced chair EYE, which included some extremely mild stretching, yogic breath-work, and tapping. As I instructed her in how to use the techniques, Mrs. Walker feigned disinterest in me and my explanations, but followed my instructions anyway. Throughout our session, she became a little less vehement and her eyes seemed livelier.

As Mrs. Walker performed Lion's Breath, she started to touch on the dissatisfaction underlying her anger and, together, we tapped it out.

Her anger dissipated slowly – like sugar dissolving in water. Eventually, over the course of several months of faithful tapping, Mrs. Walker was able to do floor-work on a yoga mat that I carried with me to her hospital room. Her transformations were further accelerated.

Her cancer treatment started to become more and more effective. She began responding to chemo and radiation. She started to feel more comfortable with her own vulnerability and to let go of the need to keep others at arm's-length with her anger.

In Reclined Cobbler's Pose, Mrs. Walker admitted her deepest fear: "If I tell people what I want, they will take it away from me."

As it turned out, her entire life had been marked by experiences of other people taking away things that Mrs. Walker loved. We tapped out all such incidents, including her memory of her mother taking away her security blanket when she was just five years old.

Mrs. Walker's daughter (whom she now referred to as "Lydia" rather than as "that ungrateful cow") reported that "It's like, as a person, she's becoming less cancerous. Mom's not mean anymore."

Mrs. Walker is now in remission, has been discharged from the hospital, and comes to see me once a month for EYE sessions. About a year into her healing journey, after her cancer had gone into remission, Mrs. Walker told me, "You can call me Grace, dear. After all, you did save my life."

Unlike Grace, I do not believe that EYE alone saved her life. In my opinion, it was EYE used in conjunction with proper medical treatment that allowed her body to heal itself. I never advise my clients to use the Emotional Yoga Experience as a substitute for appropriate medical care, but I also never suggest that they wait for this type of intervention until after finishing their treatment. In my experience, EYE can and should be used in conjunction with other interventions. The more tools that you can use to repair your body and to renovate your damaged emotions, the better off you will be. While some may point out that, with this inclusive approach to healing, it isn't clear exactly which modality causes which healing results, I don't think it matters if the goal of health is reached.

As Grace said, winking conspiratorially at me, "Who cares what did it or how it worked? All I know is that this New Age bullshit must've helped or I'd be dead right about now."

My Emotional Yoga Experience:

When I first began using EYE to transform myself and my life, my body was a war-ravaged battlefield. There had been so many casualties of my war with bulimia. I lost everything, including myself. My first Emotional Yoga Experience was by far the most transformative incident of my life.

You've heard how the willowy branches of my Tree Pose swayed as I harkened back to my childhood epilepsy. I shook. I trembled. I felt. I tapped out the fear that drove my bulimia. From that day onward, EYE became my pathway out of pain.

Again and again, I returned to the same well-trod road courtesy of my yoga mat. EYE cured me of my bulimia instantaneously. Still, I had so many other layers of dysfunction and stored emotion that I needed to let go of in order to live a fully emancipated life.

Until yoga brought me into my feelings, EFT could not bring me out of them. Despite all of my years of therapy and the mental-gymnastics that I had been going through since childhood, I had experienced energetic wounds that I couldn't reach consciously or even subconsciously (yes, I tried hypnosis). Instead, I had to heal my pain energetically.

The regular practice of EYE brought me, again and again, into self-intimacy. I began looking inward and this gave me permission to change myself from a person I could barely face in the mirror to a person I love, admire, and respect.

Over the years, I've continued to look inward. Yoga is the knock on the door of my emotions. Again and again, I swing the door open on my mat. I enter – sometimes cautiously, sometimes enthusiastically. Always, I employ my body's energy to heal itself. It is in this way that EYE continues to change my life from the inside out.

Ruth's Emotional Yoga Experience:

At fifty-three years old, Ruth was too young to feel so old. Her back seized up on an almost daily basis. She wore pain patches, kept an electric heating pad at her desk, and never left the house without her vial of prescription pain medication.

"I go to the chiropractor at least once a week," she said. "You do realize that my problems are all physical, right?"

I nodded noncommittally and shrugged my shoulders. "Let's see if we can get you to let go of some of your tension. If it helps your pain, great. If not, the worst that will happen is you'll feel more relaxed."

Appearing somewhat pacified, Ruth sank back into her chair and smiled. "I'm sorry. I'm just so frustrated," she apologized. "The pain is constant and nothing seems to help."

I had Ruth begin by gently turning her head from side-to-side, stretching the muscles in her neck.

Simply turning her head was painful. "It hurts to look around."

"What in your life does it hurt for you to look at?" I queried.

"I don't like to look at what I've missed out on. I've never been married. I've never had a family. I am fifty-three and I can't say I've ever been in love."

As her head turned on its axis, it hurt. So, too, came the painful realization that her physical pain served a purpose. It blinded her to her stored emotional angst.

In Eagle Arms, as Ruth experienced the physical tension locked in her shoulder blades, realization cut like a knife. "I'm overwhelmed at work and I hate my job. I never said it before, not even to myself, but I hate numbers and I work in finance."

The only reason Ruth got a job in finance was that her family pressured her into it. Together, we tapped out Ruth's loss of self within her family. Then, for good measure, we tapped out the actual symptoms that led Ruth to my door (back and neck pain, muscle tension, and an inability to hold chiropractic adjustments).

Ruth felt better immediately. As she strode purposefully out of her EYE session, I noticed her erect posture and straight spine. She seemed to occupy her body for the first time in a long time, maybe ever.

"I'm not sure what happened, but I feel better," Ruth told me. "I can't wait to see what happens."

What happened was incredible! Ruth's physical problems improved substantially. Her muscles and bones and joints no longer felt worn and ragged. She began to feel more and more capable of movement and even took up walking and Pilates. She has continued to see her chiropractor and now finds that her adjustments hold. She averages one visit per month now and feels great overall.

In my mind, the biggest shifts have been in the adjustments Ruth has made to her life. She decided to retire from her job in finance and to get a part-time position working at a bookstore. She's renewed her dormant passion for photography and has begun developing her own film in a darkroom that her brother helped her to build in one of her unused walk-in closets.

Ruth tells me that she has begun the process of adopting a child. She filled out all of the paperwork and has completed her application. Now, she's waiting. In the meantime, Ruth says she is exploring her own likes and dislikes. She has begun to connect with herself.

C.C.'s Emotional Yoga Experience:

C.C. hadn't been able to go to the bathroom without the aid of laxatives, enemas, stool softeners, or colonics for several years when she first came to see me for a session. She walked around with a Buddha-belly and reported feeling socially awkward because, after about a week without pooping, she'd invariably be asked if she were pregnant.

"I don't want to be around people. I literally feel like shit," C.C. told me. "This yoga crap feels pretty overwhelming. I can barely move, I feel so shitty."

Although EYE is essentially a nonverbal method of healing, language can be an interesting indicator – shedding light on both our physical and emotional experiences. C.C.'s conversation was peppered with the use of euphemisms for bowel movements and she didn't even realize it.

I had C.C. begin with a series of gentle, twisting yoga poses to stimulate the colon and to initiate the process of digestion and elimination. C.C. reported feeling stuck. Her physical stagnation made twisting poses uncomfortable. While the complaints that brought her to EYE were entirely physical, she was emotionally blocked as well.

We tapped out her physical issues of being "sick of this shit" (her words). Then, we went a layer deeper. C.C. told me in Bharadvaja's Twist, tears streaming down her face, that she had been bullied as a child. We tapped out specific instances during which C.C. was beaten up on the playground as well as her recollections of being terrorized by her older brother. While she couldn't conjure the specific memory of her brother holding her head in the toilet bowl, C.C. saw a flash of white porcelain and felt his hand on the back of her head as she touched the crown of her head to the floor in Rabbit Pose.

As she twisted her body in a Supine Spinal Twist, C.C. felt a twinge in her gut. She felt as if hands were wringing out her intestines. Remembering on the mat, C.C. recalled the many times that her parents had told her that it was her fault that she got made fun of and bullied.

Roughly twenty years later, C.C. could still hear her father telling her to "get your shit together."

Our session was scheduled for an hour and a half. Forty-five minutes into it, C.C. said, "I have to use the bathroom."

Suffice it to say, she let go of her "shit."

We spent the remainder of the session working on letting go of her childhood pain. C.C. reports no further issues with constipation. Today, instead of feeling crappy, she feels free.

Tia, Brooke, and Lester

Tia's Emotional Yoga Experience:

Tia exuded sex. She looked like a 1950s pin-up girl. Move over Marilyn Monroe! Her yoga outfit fit her like a glove. A skin-tight black bodice with a plunging neckline revealed substantial cleavage. Her dark gray leggings hugged her skin tightly and their waistband descended dangerously close to the holy grail of her femininity. Every movement that Tia made was a deliberate gesture aimed at showcasing her body. Yoga invited Tia to acknowledge the internal truths that her body contained rather than to look at her body as an object for external admiration. On the mat, Tia's body revealed that it harbored a tremendous amount of pain and shame.

In Crescent Pose, with her arms lifting skyward, she felt a wave of hope that someone might love her.

"I want a man who loves me for who I am, not for how I look."

We tapped out her belief that her only value lay in being a sex object.

It was then that Tia told me about her father: "When I was five years old, my father began coming into my room. He touched me even though at first I told him not to. I was my daddy's favorite. He made me feel special. I loved him. I had three sisters and I was the only one he molested." She stopped then, and I could tell that she was holding back.

I urged her to move into Child's Pose and to continue allowing her body to articulate her experiences.

"I've never realized this before," Tia said, her eyes beginning to water, "But I liked what my father did to me. That is so sick and so twisted."

"Talk from the place of the child," I urged her. "Don't judge it. Just feel it."

"I loved my daddy so much. It's was wrong, but it felt right."

Tia's body trembled and she began to sob. She shook her head fiercely, her blond tresses whipping around like a lash. For Tia, there was something about hurt that felt like love and something about love that felt like hurt. Until EYE, she had never acknowledged this internal rift and the dichotomy it created. She knew that her relationship history was one of abuse, but it was only with EYE that she pinpointed the source of her energetic imbalance. She associated hurt with love.

We tapped out this faulty correlation.

Tia had spent most of her adult life searching for the man who would once again make her feel like her father had made her feel – the man who would make wrong feel right, who would make her feel special even as he made her feel shame, who would both love and objectify her.

In Cobbler's Pose, Tia felt the full extent of her shame and allowed her body to say what her mind never allowed her to say, "I am ashamed because I was hurt, and ashamed because I liked it." We tapped this out.

From that session onward, Tia was empowered to seek out healthier connections. She saw that she had been using the only thing that made her feel special – her body – in an attempt to get love. However, the love never came. Tia is still single today, but the men that she dates are much healthier. Tia no longer views her body as an object to be owned, but as a vessel to be inhabited and cherished.

Brooke's Emotional Yoga Experience:

A twenty-year-old former high school prom queen, Brooke dressed like a fourteen-year-old boy. She had cut her hair short and spiky and wore oversized sweat pants and a gray hoodie. Her slim figure disappeared beneath layers of clothing – her way of insulating herself against unwanted attention. She was clearly trying to hide her beauty.

At 5'2", Brooke had a tiny, pixie-like figure. She slumped down on the yoga mat, shoulders collapsing into themselves, her back hunched over. She sat with her legs underneath her, her butt on her heels, her knees pressed tightly together. The smaller Brooke made herself physically, the more comfortable she appeared. And the more lost and dissociative.

Her PTSD was debilitating. Brooke had been raped in an alley on the way back to her dorm room after leaving a college party. Her assailants would be imprisoned for ten years, but Brooke was serving a life-sentence. She had been in therapy for two years and remained unable to let go of the endless loop of memories – their bodies on hers, the dark alley, the cell phone that had fallen from her hands and lay uselessly while her attackers held her down. She had dropped out of college following her attack and developed debilitating agoraphobia. She could not leave the house unless she was accompanied by one of her parents, and she refused to leave the house at all if it was dark outside. In fact, although Brooke lived only a fifteen minute walk away from me, her mother drove her to her session, walked her to my door, and then waited in the car while her daughter had her first EYE session.

When working with rape victims, I am always careful to have them begin by working tangentially on the trauma. I do not bring them too deeply into their bodies until they can safely navigate their memories without danger of re-traumatization. As such, I focused Brooke's first EYE session on the impact that her PTSD was having on her life in the present moment.

I geared her initial, experiential yoga poses towards body parts that tend not to store significant feelings of vulnerability or shame. To that end, the primary poses that I employed were balancing poses, shoulder openers, and gentle heart openers/backbends. My immediate goals for Brooke were to give her more balance in her life, to reduce her stress and her fear, and to help her to open her heart more fully. Yoga allowed us to look beyond Brooke's PTSD and to rescue the person that she had been before the rape.

As Brooke embarked on each pose, I asked her body to tell its stories.

One of her most monumental shifts took place during Fish Pose. As her back arched mildly, her throat opened and she began to tremble.

"What's happening?" I queried.

"I want to scream." Brooke looked confused.

"So do it."

I invited Brooke to find her voice. She erupted with a primal, bone-chilling scream. Brooke had been holding back this eruption for years. Once her throat became an open channel of expression, she let it all out. Then she tapped out her voicelessness and vulnerability.

After our first session, Brooke still refused to leave the house on her own at night or to have strangers visit her in her space, but she began venturing out on her own during the daytime, running minor errands like going to the grocery store.

It was during Brooke's second session that we began to work on her feelings before and after the rape, but not during the event. We tapped loosely around the experience. After that, I didn't hear from Brooke for over a month, but I ran into her walking her dog at the park. I looked around for her mother, but Brooke told me proudly that she had ventured out alone. Not only that, she'd been able to leave the house a dozen or so times, during the day, by herself, and a few times, at night, accompanied by her mother as long as the place that they were visiting was well-lit and the destination wasn't over-crowded by men.

By the time that she came for a third session, Brooke already felt safer and freer and we still hadn't tapped out the moment that she later identified as the source of her most powerful energetic disruption – the moment of penetration by her first attacker. It was in Staff Pose that Brooke felt a shockwave of somatic sensation.

She was so very raw, her memories so fresh, that I worked at the outer edges of the issue, like pruning an emotional hedge. Her pulse quickened. The hairs on the nape of her neck stood at attention. Every nerve ending felt as though a small shock of electricity were pulsing through her body. Beads of sweat dotted her forehead. Clearly, Brooke was remembering. Her whole body started trembling violently.

After Brooke acknowledged the roots of her fear and the fact that she was holding this emotion physically, we tapped out her fear. Brooke felt. She tapped. She did not disassociate.

Once her body articulated her fears and her energy was recalibrated, Brooke could see the world differently and move forward fearlessly. It was as if whatever seed had been spilt inside of her had taken root, sprouting a tree that grew inside of her, its gnarled and knotted branches and roots of emotional dysfunction taking over her body, mind, and soul. EYE was like a lumberjack knocking down a tree in her emotional forest. Once the incident fell away, so too did Brooke's fear, shame, and pain. Brooke has since moved out of her parents' house, re-enrolled in a different college, learned self-defense, become involved in social activism, built a social life for herself, and even started dating.

Lester's Emotional Yoga Experience:

Lester had the eyes of a cocaine addict. His gaze darted wildly around the room. Lester's wife booked his appointment for him because, as she told me, her husband had "anxiety." When he walked into his appointment, I couldn't help but think that his wife had "denial." Later on in his EYE journey, I worked with both Lester and his wife Dina, a robust yet self-effacing woman, doing couple's EYE. However, when Lester first came to see me, he and I worked individually.

Lester's intense restlessness, his constantly shifting eyes, and his perpetual hand-wringing presented me with an initial choice: Do I use his need for motion to physically engage him or do I take him into stillness to see what he's avoiding? On instinct, I chose the second approach.

I asked Lester to begin in Child's Pose. As he crouched into a ball, stretching his arms out on the mat in front of him, his hands shook. I rested my own hands gently on his back, pushing downward, subtly deepening his entry into the posture. His fingers gripped at the mat beneath them as his entire body tensed with the old, emotional residue of his childhood angst.

I have found that EYE unearths the core-level feelings behind our self-destructive behaviors and that, after releasing these emotional attachments, negative coping mechanisms vanish. In fact, it is important to note that the Emotional Yoga Experience approach to healing circumvents the need for full-disclosure, even though most of my clients end up telling me everything eventually anyway, because it operates on the body's energy system directly. Often, I get the full story in retrospect after healing has taken place. For example, "I had been smoking three packs a day, but since we started working together I've quit smoking" or "I never told you, but I was having thoughts about killing myself and they've gone away" or "I ended my affair with a married man. I realize now that I deserve more."

In Child's Pose, Lester told me that the last time that he felt safe was when he was seventeen years old, before his mother was diagnosed with cancer. As he told me the story of how, at seventeen, he became responsible for taking care of his younger brother and sister, how his mother's illness slowly ate away at her body, Lester's eyes became glassy. I coaxed him into Boat Pose, asking him to identify the emotion that he held at his core about his mother's death. It was fear. Lester said that his fear drove his anxiety.

As we tapped, I watched his energy shift. The change in Lester was palpable. As his eyes took on a sense of clarity, the lines in his face relaxed and his expression grew contemplative.

"What's going on inside of you?" I asked him. "What feelings are you experiencing?"

"I'm just remembering some things," Lester said. "I think I got a problem with coke. I'm a addict," he confessed. "I did coke the first time when I was twenty three. My momma had just died. I was at a party. I was nervous. The coke took the edge off. It make me feel like superman."

Lester seemed frozen in his memory. This time, rather than having him tap on himself, I tapped on him. (This is something that I do sometimes when working with clients who are dissociative or with children, the ill, or the elderly). Tapping directly on Lester's body, I unblocked his energy for him, allowing him to let go of his emotional attachment to the specific memory of being at a party and feeling fearful. As I did so, I fed

Lester words to repeat. He regurgitated my words, spitting them out without digesting them, repeating what I said without really understanding how or why EYE works. Lester's eyes shifted back into focus.

Next, I asked him to take Double Pigeon Pose, an intense hip-opener. Lester's hips felt incredibly tight. The cords of knotted muscle choked his joints like nooses, making Double Pigeon Pose an extremely powerful asana for him. Lester cringed as his muscles began to engage. At first, he couldn't identify what emotion his hips were holding onto, but he said that he felt physical pain and tension. We began there. I had him tap out the uncomfortable sensations. After a few rounds of tapping, Lester's face contorted into a grimace. I could tell by his expression that he had remembered something.

"When I was fourteen, my little brother get hit by a car. I was supposed to be watching him, but I wasn't paying him no mind. He run out into the street. He break his leg. I still feel guilty 'bout that. After my dad and mom get they divorce, my dad never come around much. I try to be a good older brother. After Mom die, I do what I could with Tommy. He finish high school, but never go to college. He never really became much of anything. Not that I'm anything either. My sister turn out okay for the most part, 'cept she get pregnant at fourteen. But she doing good now. Tommy can't get nothing right. But it ain't his fault. It my fault. I failed him."

Lester's guilt over not having been a better brother turned out to be at the core of his self-sabotaging behaviors. We tapped out his feelings of guilt, his belief that he did not deserve success or happiness, and his shame about not having been able to save his mother, sister, or brother.

The next time that I saw Lester was a week later. His eyes were clearer, but his face had grown even thinner. He was unshaven and disheveled. His brown eyes were brighter and the whites of his eyes were white rather than pinkish or jaundiced-looking. However, he appeared haggard. Lester told me that, after our first session, he had stopped using cocaine. His body was undergoing physical withdrawal. He felt jittery and sick. For the most part, though, whatever internal drive had compelled him to use drugs had dissipated. We focused our second session entirely around the physical symptoms that he was experiencing as a result of having stopped cold-turkey. Lester's head and body ached. He was nauseous. He sweat profusely and experienced vertigo. As for his cocaine cravings, Lester told me that he wanted to use when he woke up in the morning and right before bedtime, although he reported not having urges for the rest of the day. He hadn't succumbed to any of the urges, but the cravings were intense at these times. In Corpse Pose, Lester connected with the emotions driving his early-morning and late-night urges to use. He felt dead inside. We tapped out his internal deadness, reawakening him to life.

Our second session was primarily centered around supporting him physically and balancing his energy to facilitate physical detoxification and mitigate cravings. In Easy Pose, Lester told me that his headaches and nausea were getting in the way of him feeling at ease about his recovery. Drug-ravaged and damaged, we tapped out his physical withdrawal symptoms. Lester hasn't used since.

It has been six months and he is fully free from his compulsion to use cocaine. He also quit smoking cigarettes about a month ago. EYE powerfully affected his body and his emotions, helping him to shed his addiction as though he were a snake sloughing off his skin. Lester no longer has shifty eyes.

Margaret, Samantha, and Beth

Margaret's Emotional Yoga Experience:

Stark, imposing, and crisp, everything about Margaret seemed cold, frigid, and impersonal. It was as if she had been constructed from Lego parts, as if her body were put together with perfectly joined edges. Through EYE, it became apparent that she could be disassembled quite easily. I was there to dismantle the construction, to find the softness between the edges, to create warmth amidst the cold. Underneath her starkness, Margaret possessed a disarming sense of humor. In fact, her classically British wit had me laughing immediately.

"Dara, darling," she said conversationally, "I'm not sure that this hoodoo-voodoo will translate. I mean there is, after all, a language barrier." She winked at me.

Almost immediately, I realized that Margaret was a chameleon, donning and shedding her emotional affect depending on her audience. Years of being a diplomat's wife had conditioned her to perform, rather than live, her life. She was a riveting actress, emotionally distant but also incredibly engaging. Margaret feigned each emotional response based upon the situation, then she would slough off whatever feelings she had adopted and revert to her now-familiar state of numbness.

On the mat, Margaret stood, as frozen as a statue, her hands clutching each other as she told me her story. As the wife of a foreign diplomat, she had made a life out of wearing masks, adopting the attitudes and actions that would ingratiate her to others. She had been happy to play the role of the supporting actress, letting her husband shine in the spotlight.

She idolized him so much that, as she said, "I frankly lost myself to that royal wanker. I had no sense of where I ended and he began."

Nine years into their marriage, Margaret walked in on her husband and his secretary having sex in their bedroom. Once she discovered her husband's betrayal, she dug deeper and uncovered a history of infidelities in his past.

"It was all a farce." Margaret shrugged her shoulders backward in Mountain Pose. "When I found out, something inside of me froze. It was like my heart froze."

Margaret's yoga postures were a reflection of every aspect of her life – sharp, angular, and hard. I have never seen a more perfect Triangle Pose.

I tried to bring pliability and flexibility into her body and the result was that she began to feel. Deep within her long-frozen chest dwelled a pain that she had never allowed herself to acknowledge. With each flowing motion, Margaret began to melt deeper into her emotions. Her main emotion – the emotion beneath all of the others – was fear. At the core of her emotional iceberg lay the fear of ever opening herself to love again. Because she had been so deeply wounded, Margaret's energy had been short-circuited. Margaret had shut off the connection to her internal emotional wiring and, without yoga to reopen the door to her emotions, would not have been able to access any feelings – positive or negative.

In Sphinx Pose, by peeling open her heart, Margaret felt how constricted she had become. As she expanded her physical chest, opening her heart, she confronted how closed off she was from giving and receiving love. It was only through rebalancing her body's energy that she could let love in and let go of her physical and emotional barriers to integrating love into her life.

Immediately after our session, Margaret reported feeling lighter. A few weeks later, she called me, not to schedule a session, but to update me on her situation.

"I have been laughing," Margaret said cheerily. "I've been laughing so much I can scarcely believe it. Bloody hell, I even went to a comedy club. And I saw a sad movie on the telly last week and cried. I'm not dead inside anymore. I have feelings. Also, I did something sort of naughty this week," Margaret said.

Across the phone line, I could almost hear the mischievous upturn of her mouth forming a smirk, "My ex-husband left some of his things in my attic when he moved out. I decided that my house is much too cold these days, so I burned his clothes and books and papers in my fireplace. I think that, maybe, I was angry. I'm not angry anymore, though."

I found myself laughing as I hung up the phone. Clearly, the ice had thawed.

Samantha's Emotional Yoga Experience:

Folds of fabric hung off of her body, as if they could conceal her excess weight. Samantha's eyes had receded into her face, swallowed by the layers of her flab. Her body was a swollen mass of loose flesh. Layers of chalky foundation pooled in the crevices around her mouth and flaked within the creases of the crow's feet wrinkling around her eyes. She popped a piece of gum in her mouth and began chomping. Her dark lips, looking like she had smeared them with raspberry jelly, moved in slow-motion as she opened her mouth to introduce herself.

"Samantha Starwell," she shook my hand. "It's wonderful to meet you." She had a loud, lugubrious voice, which flowed like poured liquid.

"What brings you here?" I asked Samantha.

"I'm eating myself to death," she told me. "I've tried Weight Watchers, Jenny Craig, exercise, vegetarianism, fasting, Atkins, you name it. I've lost and gained more pounds than I can count. Lately, I've been unable to stop eating for more than an hour at a time. When I'm not eating, I'm chewing gum. I have to have something in my mouth every second of the day."

I could have guessed as much. I had seen Samantha stuff a donut into her mouth on the way from her car to my door.

Samantha sat on her mat, propped by a pillow. Her first breakthrough arose in Easy Pose.

"Eating hides my vulnerability," she finally verbalized the truth.

Bundles of fat spilling out of her pants, breathing heavily, ruddy-cheeked, chewing gum because she couldn't stop eating, Samantha's fat both insulated and entrapped her.

"Food makes me feel safe," she realized.

As Samantha's body unfolded, so too did her story. She had been a compulsive overeater since before she could remember. One of ten children, she had grown up feeling invisible and liking that feeling. Disappearing within a family of loud, boisterous siblings became Samantha's way of insulating herself from the outside world. All of Samantha's siblings and both of her parents were overweight, but, tipping the scales at 300 pounds, Samantha was by far the most severely obese member of her family.

In Child's Pose, Samantha recalled feeling scared throughout most of her youth. Her mother and father had already raised eight children by the time Samantha was born.

"My sisters kind of raised me, but they had their own lives to live. I remember a lot of skinned knees and broken bones from playing with the older kids. After a while, I stopped playing with them. I stayed home and ate candy and read books about other people's adventures."

Through EYE, Samantha connected with her body. She actively listened to its messages as it explained that eating offered her a physical sensation of safety. Food provided insulation against a world which offered her no protection, or so her body told her. Together, we tapped out her feelings about food. Samantha's obsession with eating diminished.

After that first session, Samantha felt safer in her own skin. As we've worked together, she's experienced steady weight loss. She no longer has to have something in her mouth constantly. And, so far, she's lost 97 pounds!

Beth's Emotional Yoga Experience:

A bundle of nervous energy, thin and wiry, Beth's mind seemed to flit from thought to thought. She explained that she felt like she was coming completely unglued. A few days earlier, she had gotten lost while driving and had pulled over on the side of the road and wept. Beth told me that she felt hopeless in every area of her life.

Beth had been doing yoga for years and loved the benefits she got from yoga's stillness and silence. Despite her tendency towards anxiety, she felt a tremendous amount of relief during each yoga class. However, Beth told me that she avoided some back-bending and heart-opening poses altogether because they made her weepy and morose.

Needless to say, I had her begin in Bridge Pose. As Beth crossed over the bridge of her emotions, she traveled from the pain of the present back into her past. She heard her daughter's words and felt their harsh impact reverberating through her entire body. Beth felt like a failure as a mother.

Together, we tapped out her memory.

Throughout her session, as Beth opened her heart and bent her back, the following issues came to light: Beth thought that she was a failure because her marriage hadn't lasted; she was still in love with her ex-husband although they had divorced twenty years earlier; she believed herself to be a horrible mother and inadequate grandmother; and she had been raped as a teenager and, as a result, had always felt unlovable.

Each of these issues was a layer of Beth's emotional onion, requiring its own EYE sequencing. After identifying each of these stored feelings, I had Beth delve deeper into her emotions while we recalibrated her physical energy. She cried before and during each round of tapping, but Beth reported experiencing an immediate emotional lightness after a few short rounds of tapping.

Since that first session, six months ago, Beth reports that she now has a much healthier relationship with her daughter, and has even been able to set boundaries with her. Beth also told me that she is no longer pining for her ex-husband. In fact, she finally discarded his old belongings that she had been holding on to. She said that not only does she now feel lovable, but she feels loved. Beth has even started dating! Prior to her session, she had not been on a date since her divorce over twenty years ago.

Surprisingly, Beth told me that her insulin levels have also improved. She is diabetic and, while she didn't disclose this at the time of our initial consultation, she told me that her insulin levels have been consistently more stable since our session together despite the fact that she has made no other changes to her lifestyle, diet or exercise.

She reported that her anxiety levels are still high, but, since we hadn't worked directly on this issue, Beth plans to come back for a session that will deal specifically with her anxiety.

The progression from emotion to emancipation is easy and effective. As the stories of Holly, Lisa, Tim, Vanessa, Jennifer, Kristin, Morgan, Lori, Maureen, Mrs. Walker, Ruth, C.C., Tia, Brooke, Lester, Margaret, Samantha, and Beth reveal, EYE uncovers our bodies' emotional truths and provides an energetic pathway to healing and wholeness.

Through my many years as an active bulimic, thousands of hours on therapist's couches, and years as an EYE practitioner, I've learned this: ***Our bodies, not our minds, are our best allies in our war against negative feelings.*** The most effective way to reset our emotions is to physically diagnose and treat those issues. Please do not misunderstand this. I am not invalidating our mental faculties; in fact, on some level, our minds can be too smart for their own good.

Because our minds want desperately to establish a rational basis for our feelings, they often minimize our emotional experiences. Our bodies, on the other hand, only know how they feel, what they want; where they are in pain, what is pleasurable and what they need physically. Sometimes, when we fail to listen to our bodies, we fail to articulate the physical or emotional pain occurring within us, because of our mind-body disconnect.

As you've seen from the case histories described within this book, the effect of utilizing the wisdom of our bodies, through physical introspection, was that each client moved beyond his or her old, self-limiting beliefs. Through the Emotional Yoga Experience, each underwent an entire paradigm shift. Their dimness changed to vibrancy. Likewise, I invite you to develop your own experiential relationship with this text as you forge your own physical and emotional connection. Step into your body, through the physical discipline of yoga, and step out of your negative emotions and actions, using EFT.

Emancipate: Live a Happy, Healthy Life with EYE

A beautiful, bouncing, baby boy, Vanessa's son can never make up for the fact that Vanessa lost her daughter. He doesn't have to. She loves him for who he is, not as a replacement for his deceased sibling. While she loved Laurel, too, her life does not revolve around her dead daughter. Today, Vanessa is free to focus her attention on her living child. Her son is a smiling beacon of all of her hopes and dreams – the fruit born of her once-bereft womb.

Like most of my clients, her Emotional Yoga Experience has opened Vanessa up to the joy of life. The technique cannot eradicate our pasts. Why would we want it to? Instead, it softens our emotional edges; it unlocks the prisons of our own minds and frees our bodies from their stored pain.

One of the incredible aspects about each person's Emotional Yoga Experience is that it offers them a unique pathway to discovering who they are and how they want to live, free of old self-limiting beliefs. For example, Lisa may not have ever become a professional dancer, but she has developed an embodied existence. She moves through life now with self-confidence. Although her mother never allowed her to express herself, each time that Lisa takes a Zumba class, she "shakes what her momma gave her." Tim's closeted existence was soul-crushing. Today, he no longer feels like he has to hide his homosexuality. He has found peace with himself and his sexual orientation.

Addictive behaviors lose their grasp as we connect with our bodies and reset our emotional attachments. I'm my own best case-history, having stopped a twelve-year cycle of self-abuse in a single EYE session. Many of my clients, while their results have taken a bit more time, have been able to find release from their own self-injurious behavioral patterns. Morgan has stopped drinking and cutting herself. Her body no longer functions as a receptacle for violence. She appreciates herself and is free from the compulsion to self-harm. She respects her body too much to hurt it.

Lester quit using cocaine. Admittedly, that is not the problem that brought him to me. The cocaine-anxiety connection existed in a chicken-and-egg relationship. His emotional and behavioral turmoil were inextricably linked. What about Lester's anxiety? He says that he generally feels calm nowadays. This does not mean that he is completely worry-free, but his constant undercurrent of fear is gone. Instead, he feels specific apprehension tied to a particular circumstance, and when the situation ends the anxiety goes with it. For example, he recently felt a bit of nervous trepidation when sitting with his manager for his yearly employee-evaluation. He did well, however, and his nervousness lost its edge a few minutes into the meeting. This is a far-cry from the darting-eyed, coke-fueled, worry-wart that Lester used to be. Additionally, as a direct result of their couples EYE sessions, he and his wife, Dina, have experienced tremendous healing in their relationship. Lester has stopped blaming Dina for things that are not her fault and she has stopped trying to fix his problems. Each of them has, on their own, cultivated self-acceptance and has also learned to accept his/her mate. Their marriage is the strongest that it has ever been.

Even when unencumbered by addictions, people can feel weighted down by pain. Emotional encumbrances impact them on a daily basis and diminish their ability to experience joy. Shame, guilt, self-hatred, depression, and anxiety infiltrate our minds and deposit themselves in our bodies, and it is only by accessing our stored pain and releasing it physically that radical transformations can occur – first, on the mat, then, in our lives.

Tia let go of her shame. She will always be an incest survivor and her past will never be a cause for celebration, but Tia now understands that her father's misdeeds belong to him. The axis of blame rests with him. Today, Tia acknowledges that she loved her father and that he raped her, but she doesn't love him because he raped her. That distinction has enabled her to internalize the self-forgiveness that she had been able to comprehend cognitively, but, until EYE, had not understood emotionally. What's more, EYE freed Tia to gravitate towards a higher caliber of man.

These days, Brooke's mother, like other mothers of many college-aged girls, often wonders what her daughter is doing. Unlike other mothers, this not knowing is a welcome change for her. Her daughter is no longer cowering beneath the covers or sitting, forlorn on the couch unwilling to venture beyond the comfort zone of their family's home. Brooke lives on her own now. She is no longer a prisoner of her past. In fact, she is using her trauma to help others in their fight against violence perpetrated against women. She has become an activist for others and for herself.

The frost around Margaret's heart has thawed. No longer an automaton, she experiences a full spectrum of emotions and has been reawakened to life through EYE. Samantha has lost a great deal since she started EYE. She has lost her feeling of invisibility and her reliance on food. She has lost her uneasy apprehension, her feelings of inadequacy, and, most noticeably, she has lost 97 pounds to date.

While this book was primarily concerned with addressing emotional issues, EYE works on a physical level as well. Remember, C.C. finally pooped. She continues to have regular bowel movements and feels unencumbered by old, emotional waste.

Each of the clients described in this book arrived at my door feeling lost. Intellectually, the majority of them thought that they knew what their issues were. Most had tried various conventional interventions to get well. Emotionally, and energetically, they all remained stuck. EYE was the missing link between their brains and their bodies. It fused their emotional and intuitive intelligences. With the body-based diagnosis that yoga offers and the energetic transformation afforded by EFT, these clients rewrote their emotional histories. They are no longer imprisoned by their pasts.

Because we operate in the purview of our minds, all of us are limited in our ability to self-diagnose our own emotional issues. Each time that we experience a negative emotion, it is the direct result of our bodies' energy system being out of balance. The experiences of healing contained within this book clearly reveal the inherent limitations of cognitive self-diagnosis. Our bodies contain memories, feelings, experiences, and truths that we can only hear if we actively engage them in conversation.

Through yoga, we interrogate our bodies, asking them questions. By allowing our physical selves to find their voices, and to express their experiences, we begin to accurately diagnose our emotional issues. As our bodies articulate their emotions, we are then left with the painful truth: yoga brings us to our problems, but it does not offer us solutions. Where, then, does that leave us? Are we doomed to forever repeat the same destructive behavioral and emotional patterns? No. Because, in addition to diagnosing our issues, our bodies offer us solutions – the energetic repair of our negative emotions. Again, yoga alone is not enough. The body, however, holds the key to our healing. The resolution that it offers exists beyond the scope of yogic self-inquiry. It is energetic.

This leads us to EFT – a safe, effective, results-oriented technique used to repair our bodies' disrupted energy systems and to resolve emotional issues rapidly and permanently. Like a technician restoring electricity during a power-outage, EFT resets our emotional energy, illuminating us to positive feelings. It is easy and effective. Where can we find our emotional "reset" buttons? Simple. EFT offers us a systematic technique of meridian-tapping complete with all of the points that we need in order to achieve this physical attunement. EFT is an energetic approach to recalibrating our bodies' energy systems; however, I have found that it sometimes misses the mark. Even though it works by rebalancing our bodies' energy system, this technique typically relies on a cognitive diagnosis. EFT is a verbal, rational discipline developed by an engineer. The Emotional Yoga Experience (EYE), on the other hand, offers a nonverbal, body-oriented, experiential approach to healing that often defies logic. Drawing upon the foundations of yogic self-inquiry, EYE trusts our bodies to both diagnose and heal themselves.

The Next Steps:

You have read about yoga, felt your feelings, connected with your body's stored emotions, reconnected your energetic wiring, and learned about yoga and EFT. You have forged an experiential relationship with your body, both diagnosing and treating your emotional imbalances physically, and have begun to experience the benefits of EYE. You have followed the evolution of eighteen of my clients as they traveled their own EYE paths, and you have read some of my personal healing history. No doubt, you have engaged with the various exercises provided herein and have begun to reap the benefits of EYE in your life.

So where does that leave you? Now what?

This section marks the beginning of your own Emotional Yoga Experience transformation. Think of this segment as your introduction to yourself. What can you expect now? Anticipate the unexpected. Each person's EYE is individual because each person's body holds different emotions and experiences. Additionally, the same person may retain different feelings and release different stored energy based upon where they are in the moment, on the mat. I want to give you more than information, more than sample exercises. I want to give you your own, prescriptive EYE session aimed at diagnosing and treating your individual emotional and behavioral issues. Use the following section to begin to live the life that you were meant to live. As I take you through your first full EYE session, you will use your body's intuitive intelligence to diagnose and treat the issues that have been ailing you.

Before reading on, make sure that you have the following:

- Comfortable yoga-type clothing
- A pen or pencil
- Loose-leaf paper or a journal. Feel free to write directly in the spaces provided in this book. However, as you may want to re-use the session multiple times, writing your answers somewhere else may be useful. You may also consider photocopying the session pages and using, and re-using, your copies.
- A yoga mat
- A quiet space in which to conduct your EYE
- A box of tissues (in case you feel a need to cry)
- About an hour and a half of free time in which to transform your life and your emotions from the inside out. Remember, you can break up the following session into shorter segments if you choose and you need not complete the session in a single sitting.

When I see a client for an EYE session, I integrate yoga and EFT as a dynamic-duo, bringing my clients into a pose, excavating whatever stored emotions their body has been retaining, then freeing them immediately from their emotional wounds by employing the EFT tapping technique right away. There is no reading or writing involved because I act as the body's interrogator and liberator, diagnosing each client's retained emotional wounds with questions that I ask based on the moment and focused on them as an individual. As such, each EYE session is spontaneously expressive and is not cognitively-based.

Without the luxury of having me in your living room guiding you through your own experiences on the mat, you can still derive all of the healing benefits of EYE. However, you will have to work a bit differently. This EYE session is structured much like a remote EYE prescription, which I write when working with clients who live far away from me. It will require you to delve into your own body's wisdom as you enter each yoga pose while asking yourself targeted questions designed to unearth the emotions that are clogging up your energy flow. You can do as I do with a client – entering an emotion with yoga and immediately restoring your positive emotional flow with EFT – or, as you move through your own Emotional Yoga Experience, you may want to work a bit differently. Maybe you will want to take one pose and one question at a time, tapping as you go. Maybe you will feel more comfortable moving through all of the inward-looking yoga postures and associated questions in an emotional series, answering all of the questions and identifying the issues first, then going back and tapping out each of the issues that you have identified. You can modify this approach based on your individual needs and preferences.

I suggest that you do not move ahead from one Emotional Yoga Experience series to the next without having completed the previous one, by which I mean the yoga posture, questions, answers, and tapping. My reason for this is that your body is best served by resetting your attachment to one emotion (i.e. shame, fear, sadness, etc.) before moving on to the next emotion. This approach of not skipping too far ahead will keep you rooted in the physical, experiential aspects of your healing evolution and keep you from becoming too cerebral. On that note, as you respond to each question, keep your answers brief, responding in note-form, rather than writing long explanations.

If you are short on time, it is perfectly fine to do one segment one day and another segment another day. It is also entirely acceptable to begin with a later section, then go backward to a previous step. Feel free to skip around. Feel free to begin with the section that you are the most drawn to or the most resistant to. Remember,

EYE is a technique that is aimed at your own personal needs and requirements. Hopefully, by the time that you arrive at this point in this book, you will know yourself well enough to intuitively decide which approach will work best for you. I encourage you to hold onto the following EYE session and to revisit it periodically in order to facilitate your continual emotional evolution.

Remember, in conducting your very first EYE session, that there is not one "right" way to practice EYE. There is only your way. Meet yourself where you are, step onto your mat and begin. Allow this book to act as your manual for self-transformation. Read it voraciously, reread it, use and reuse the techniques offered here. Go inward, again and again, and your outward experiences will improve. As you embark upon your new, empowered existence, you will feel better and your life will improve substantially. You can use this book in place of more traditional approaches or as an adjunct to other modalities. Your body is its own best diagnostician and healer, and you are the person best qualified to determine how to incorporate EYE into your healing repertoire. I urge you to engage with this text and to explore for yourself what works in terms of integrating EYE into your life.

As you move forward, I want to make note of an important point: **The goal of EYE is not to stop you from feeling your feelings.** Emotions are a wonderful part of our human experience. I would never want to deprive anyone of the full spectrum of feelings that comprise our existence. As a member of the human race, you should feel joy, love, anger, sadness, hope, empathy, connection, vulnerability, fear, and a range of all of the emotions. I hope that you will feel all of your feelings – some "negative," some "positive." If we do not experience the natural ebb-and-flow of feelings, we miss out on the rich contrast that comes with shifting emotions. For instance, experiencing joy on the heels of sadness is like the richly-rewarding phenomenon of marveling over the blooming of spring crocuses after a long, cold, barren winter.

All of your emotions have an appropriate place and it is never "wrong" to feel. There are times when negative emotions are appropriate. The problem arises when the duration of an emotion extends beyond the scope of an experience. By this, I mean that if you are mildly nervous about an upcoming math test and that minor angst compels you to study, then your apprehension is useful and fitting. If you are still anxious about your math test four days after having taken it, your emotional barometer is out-of-balance. If you think about your emotions as energy flowing along a pathway, then the life cycle of each emotion should be short-lived. Ideally, a feeling will come over you, run through you, and then be released. A new feeling then comes in and takes its place. Problems occur when the only emotions that we feel are negative, when our emotional responses feel disproportionate to the situation, when we get stuck in one emotional state, or when we can't feel much of anything at all. EYE won't deaden you to your emotions. Instead, it will enliven you to your feelings – all of them – and it will enable your emotions to flow freely within you. Life is anything but stagnant and, as such, our feelings should be dynamic and energizing rather than fixed and depressing.

Overall, the issue is one of impact. The object is for your positive emotions to have a lasting impression upon you and for you to feel your negative emotions fleetingly. While EYE will not strip you of the spectrum of your feelings, it will enable you to live within the field of your positive emotional energy most of the time. You will start to feel good about your life and about yourself. Negative emotions will no longer color the lens through which you view the world. Instead, through EYE, you will envision your life with a new, happier perspective and see yourself with a new, more self-actualizing worldview. You can let go of any physical, mental, and emotional barriers standing in your way. You can open yourself up to joy. With EYE, you can embrace your body and reclaim your own personal power.

As motion unearths emotion and you reset your energetic equilibrium, delve into the stored feelings contained within your body, explore the terrain of your feelings, cultivate contentment, weed out stored negative energy, and plant positive emotions. Remember the initial image of you sitting, trembling in the darkness of your emotional room? With each Emotional Yoga Experience, I invite you to flip the switch from "off" to "on" and to see yourself and your life differently. You have been living in the darkness for too long. I invite you to shine radiantly. Namaste means the light in me honors the light in you. Welcome to the light. Namaste.

Now, let's pretend that you are a client who has just walked through my door.

Welcome to your first EYE session.

Your First Emotional Yoga Experience (EYE) Session

The following is a step-by-step Emotional Yoga Experience sample session designed to provide you with emotional relief on multiple levels. These instructional exercises are general enough to rapidly resolve a number of broad-based emotional issues, and specific enough to offer you your own personal path of positive transformation.

REMINDER: Allow your body to answer, rather than your mind. Write down the first answer that comes up and tap out whatever issues arise.

STRESS SERIES

Easy Pose

Come to sit on your mat. You may want to put a folded blanket or a yoga block underneath your buttocks for comfort. Cross your legs, slipping one foot in front of the other, and place your feet below your knees. Bend your knees and allow them to drop out to the sides. Ideally, your knees will come below your hips. Keep your head and body straight. As you sit in Easy Pose, with your spine erect, close your eyes and take several slow, deep breaths. Feel the discomfort arise within you. Ask yourself: **What in my life today causes me the most uneasiness?** Write down your answer(s). You should note that one issue may come to the surface, or you may have several things come to mind. Jot down the first problem(s) that your body reveals.

I am uneasy because ____

____

Use your answer(s) above to fill in the tapping phrases below. Tap out the issue(s) that arise following the three-step EFT tapping method (the Setup, the Sequence, and Repeat the Sequence). For a reminder of how to tap, see the EFT tapping sequence located at the end of this chapter.

"Even though I am uneasy because ______________________________,
I deeply and completely love and accept myself."

"Even though I am uneasy because ______________________________,
I deeply and completely love and accept myself."

"Even though I am uneasy because ______________________________,
I deeply and completely love and accept myself."

Prayer Palms

Continue to sit in Easy Pose. Bring your palms together at your heart center, in front of your chest, as if you were praying. While this pose is typically gentle and meditative, for our purposes, I invite you to press your palms together as firmly as you can for as long as you can. This steady union of palm against palm will immediately dredge up sensations in your hands, arms, and shoulders. Feel your hands vibrate with tension. Focus on the accumulated stress and pressure that you experience in your everyday life. Draw your attention to the building force of your palms pressing together, allowing the physical sensation to act as a mirror for the tension accumulating in your life. Experience the emotions that arise. Ask yourself: **What in my life today causes me the most stress/pressure?** Write down your answer(s). You should note that one issue may come to the surface, or you may have several things come to mind. Jot down the first problem(s) that your body reveals.

I feel stressed/pressured because ____

____

Use your answer(s) above to fill in the tapping phrases below. Tap out the issue(s) that arise following the three-step EFT tapping method (the Setup, the Sequence, and Repeat the Sequence). For a reminder of how to tap, see the EFT tapping sequence located at the end of this chapter.

"Even though I feel stress/pressure because ________________________________,
I deeply and completely love and accept myself."

"Even though I feel stress/pressure because ________________________________,
I deeply and completely love and accept myself."

"Even though I feel stress/pressure because ________________________________,
I deeply and completely love and accept myself."

STRESS RESPONSE SERIES

Cat/Cow Poses

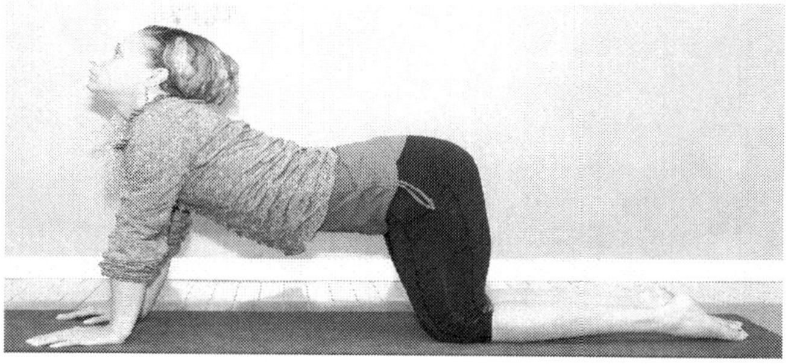

Begin on your hands and knees, positioning your knees directly beneath your hips and your hands directly beneath your shoulders. Keep your back straight. Consider this your "neutral" position. As you exhale, round your back as you gaze at your belly, arching like a cat. Then, as you inhale, dip your hips downward and sink your abdomen, creating a downward curvature of the spine (the opposite of Cat Pose). This is called Cow Pose. Move between Cat and Cow Poses, rounding the back and gazing towards the belly on the exhalation and dipping the abdomen downward and turning the face skyward on each inhalation. Initiate the movement from your spine as you shift between these two poses, transitioning from Cat to Cow. Feel the opposing sensations of opening and closing. While undulating your spine, looking upward then downward, allow yourself to identify which sensation feels more comfortable for you. Notice if expanding your heart (in Cow Pose) feels better or if you prefer curling inward (in Cat Pose). Ask yourself: **Am I more comfortable opening up or closing off?** Circle your answer below:

I feel more comfortable opening up/closing off.
Tap out your answer using the setup phrase below.

"Even though I feel more comfortable when I am opening up/closing off, and even though I struggle with opening up/closing off, I deeply and completely love and accept myself."

How does your physical experience relate to your experiences in life? If you are more comfortable closing off and are uncomfortable opening up, ask yourself: **Where in my life do I close myself off from others?**

If you are more comfortable opening up and are uncomfortable curling inward, ask yourself: **Where in my life do I go outside of myself for validation and struggle when I have to look to myself for solace?**

Write down your answer(s). You should note that one issue may come to the surface, or you may have several things come to mind. Jot down the first problem(s) that your body reveals.

I close myself off from others by ____

____

I go outside of myself for validation and resist self-validation when ____________________

____

Use your answer(s) above to fill in the tapping phrases below. Tap out the issue(s) that arise following the three-step EFT tapping method (the Setup, the Sequence, and Repeat the Sequence). For a reminder of how to tap, see the EFT tapping sequence located at the end of this chapter.

"Even though I close myself off by ____,

I deeply and completely love and accept myself."

"Even though I close myself off by ____,
I deeply and completely love and accept myself."

"Even though I close myself off by ____,
I deeply and completely love and accept myself."

"Even though I go outside of myself for validation and resist validating myself when ______________
____,
I deeply and completely love and accept myself."

"Even though I go outside of myself for validation and resist validating myself when ______________
____,
I deeply and completely love and accept myself."

"Even though I go outside of myself for validation and resist validating myself when ______________
____,
I deeply and completely love and accept myself."

Identify one specific example from your past of a time when you closed yourself off to others when you wanted to open up, or one example of an incident when you were too reliant on others when you would rather have listened to yourself or met your own needs. Write down your answer(s). You should note that one issue may come to the surface, or you may have several things come to mind. Jot down the first problem(s) that your body reveals.

I closed myself off from ______________________ (include specific name/names) when _________
____

I was too reliant on __________________________(include specific name/names) and did not listen to myself when ____

Use your answer(s) above to fill in the tapping phrases below. Tap out the issue(s) that arise following the three-step EFT tapping method (the Setup, the Sequence, and Repeat the Sequence). For a reminder of how to tap, see the EFT tapping sequence located at the end of this chapter.

"Even though I closed myself off from ____
when ____, I deeply and completely love and accept myself."

"Even though I was too reliant on ____
when ____, and even though I wish I had listened to myself and trusted myself, I deeply and completely love and accept myself."

GRIEF/SADNESS SERIES

Pigeon Pose (right leg)

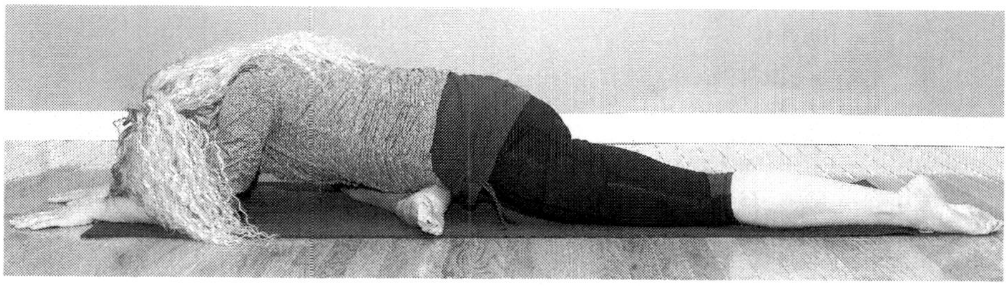

Come into a tabletop position, on all fours with your knees below your hips. Slide your right ankle forward, behind your left wrist. Your right leg will bend and your right shin will be beneath your torso. Stretch your left leg behind you on your yoga mat. Fold forward, allowing the weight of your body over the right leg to intensify the stretch in your right hip. As you feel the deep opening in your hips, tune in to your physical and emotional experiences. With each exhalation, go deeper into the stored tension in the musculature of your hip-joint. Ask yourself: **What loss am I grieving?** Write down your answer(s). You should note that one issue may come to the surface, or you may have several things come to mind. Jot down the first problem(s) that your body reveals.

I am grieving the loss of ____

____

Use your answer(s) above to fill in the tapping phrases below. Tap out the issue(s) that arise following the three-step EFT tapping method (the Setup, the Sequence, and Repeat the Sequence). For a reminder of how to tap, see the EFT tapping sequence located at the end of this chapter.

"Even though I am grieving the loss of __________________________________,
I deeply and completely love and accept myself."

"Even though I am grieving the loss of __________________________________,
I deeply and completely love and accept myself."

"Even though I am grieving the loss of __________________________________,
I deeply and completely love and accept myself."

Pigeon Pose (left leg)

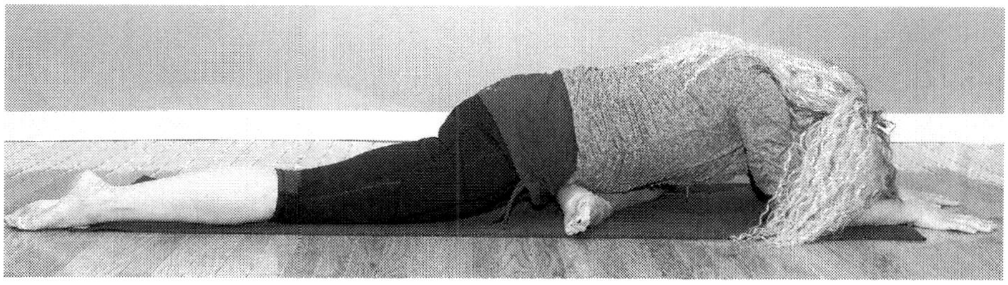

Enter into this pose in the same way that you did Pigeon Pose on the right side, except this time slide your left ankle behind your right wrist, bend your left leg and bring your left shin beneath your torso. Experience the sensations in your hips. With each exhalation, go deeper into the stored tension in the musculature of your hip-joint. Feel whatever emotions arise within you. Ask yourself: **What causes me the most sadness in my life?** Write down your answer(s). You should note that one issue may come to the surface, or you may have several things come to mind. Jot down the first problem(s) that your body reveals.

I am sad because ____

____

Use your answer(s) above to fill in the tapping phrases below. Tap out the issue(s) that arise following the three-step EFT tapping method (the Setup, the Sequence, and Repeat the Sequence). For a reminder of how to tap, see the EFT tapping sequence located at the end of this chapter.

"Even though I am sad because ______________________________,
I deeply and completely love and accept myself."

"Even though I am sad because ______________________________,
I deeply and completely love and accept myself."

"Even though I am sad because ______________________________,
I deeply and completely love and accept myself."

Modified Pigeon Pose (both sides)

Begin by lying on your back with your knees bent and tucked in towards your chest. Cross your right ankle over your left knee, flexing both feet. Threading your arms in between your legs, take hold of the back of your left thigh with both hands and gently hug your left leg in towards your body. With your ankle crossed over your knee, feel the stored sensation in your hips and allow your body to experience its discomfort. Experience the feelings that spring to the surface. After remaining in this pose for several breath cycles, switch the orientation of your legs, crossing your left ankle over your right knee. Again, connect with your emotions. As you perform Modified Pigeon Pose on both sides, engaging each hip individually, allow your body to tune into the ways in which you attempt to modulate your grief. Ask yourself: **What negative/unhealthy behavior do I use to cope with my grief?** Write down your answer(s). You should note that one issue may come to the surface, or you may have several things come to mind. Jot down the first problem(s) that your body reveals.

I cope with my grief/sadness by ____

____

Use your answer(s) above to fill in the tapping phrases below. Tap out the issue(s) that arise following the three-step EFT tapping method (the Setup, the Sequence, and Repeat the Sequence). For a reminder of how to tap, see the EFT tapping sequence located at the end of this chapter.

"Even though I cope with my grief/sadness by ______________________________,
I deeply and completely love and accept myself."

"Even though I cope with my grief/sadness by ______________________________,
I deeply and completely love and accept myself."

"Even though I cope with my grief/sadness by ______________________________,
I deeply and completely love and accept myself."

Double Pigeon Pose (both sides)

Double Pigeon Pose (also known as Fire Log Pose) is an intense hip opener that will likely flood your body with physical sensations. It can be an extremely emotionally evocative pose, carrying with it the potential to uncork long bottled-up feelings. Sit on your yoga mat. Slide your left foot beneath your right leg, to the outside of your right hip, and lay the outer leg upon your mat. Stack your right shin on top of your left. Flex both feet and line up your feet with your knees. Walk your hands forward, bending over your legs, opening your groin and your hips as you fold forward. Spend time deepening your entry into this powerful pose by breathing deeply and holding the posture for several rounds of breath. Let the physical release in the hip excavate emotions that you have been holding onto. Take Double Pigeon Pose on the other side, again focusing upon the sensations of opening in your hips. Allow each side of your body to articulate its own experience. Make sure to engage both of your hips by alternating sides while experiencing the resulting physical and emotional sensations. Focus on the things in your life that intensify your sadness. Ask yourself: **What intensifies my sadness/grief? What do I do that makes my sadness/grief worse?** Write down your answer(s). You should note that one issue may come to the surface, or you may have several things come to mind. Jot down the first problem(s) that your body reveals.

My grief/sadness becomes even more intense when ______________________________

____

Use your answer(s) (above) to fill in the tapping phrases (below). Tap out the issue(s) that arise following the three-step EFT tapping method (the Setup, the Sequence, and Repeat the Sequence). For a reminder of how to tap, see the EFT tapping sequence located at the end of this chapter.

"Even though ____
____ makes my grief even worse,
I deeply and completely love and accept myself."

"Even though ____
____ makes my grief even worse,
I deeply and completely love and accept myself."

"Even though ____
____ makes my grief even worse,
I deeply and completely love and accept myself."

Downward Dog

Come to hands and knees on your yoga mat, with your knees directly underneath your hips and your hands slightly in front of your shoulders. Curl your toes under, pressing your hands firmly downward on the mat. Straighten your arms and legs, lengthening your tailbone and broadening your back. Your body will form an upside down V-shape. With your palms pressing down into your mat and your heels intending downward, imagine that the base of your spine contains all of your accumulated depression. Visualize your spinal column as a coil of sadness – radiating from your tailbone into your limbs. Imagine that you could expel all of your stored depression out of your body and release it into your mat, letting your sorrows flow out of you and into the light to be looked at and let go of. As you remain in Downward Dog, connect with a specific memory of a disappointing event or a depressive episode from your past. Ask yourself: **When was I depressed? Why was I so sad?** Write down your answer(s). You should note that one issue may come to the surface, or you may have several things come to mind. Jot down the first problem(s) that your body reveals.

I was depressed when ____

____

I was depressed because ____

____

Use your answer(s) above to fill in the tapping phrases below. Tap out the issue(s) that arise following the three-step EFT tapping method (the Setup, the Sequence, and Repeat the Sequence). For a reminder of how to tap, see the EFT tapping sequence located at the end of this chapter.

"Even though I was depressed when ____,
I deeply and completely love and accept myself."

"Even though I was depressed when ____,
I deeply and completely love and accept myself."

"Even though I was depressed when ____,
I deeply and completely love and accept myself."

"Even though I was depressed because ______________________________,
I deeply and completely love and accept myself."

"Even though I was depressed because ______________________________,
I deeply and completely love and accept myself."

"Even though I was depressed because ______________________________,
I deeply and completely love and accept myself."

ANGER SERIES

Breath of Fire

By forcing your diaphragm in and out, Breath of Fire directly impacts your navel center, flushing out toxins as well as emotions. Sit on your heels. Breathe in and out through your nose. As you exhale, pull your abdomen in sharply towards your diaphragm and, as you inhale, expand your belly. Breath of Fire is, as the name suggests, a very fast-paced breathing exercise. As you do this, breathe loudly and audibly. When perfected, the rate of each breath cycle should be roughly 2-3 times per second (120-180 times per minute). Try to work up to a minute of continuous, rapid-fire breathing as you connect with your stored anger. Visualize the person, place, or thing that causes you the most anger as you rapidly expel your breath. Forcefully pump your navel for between 30 seconds and 1 minute, all the while visualizing the person, place, or thing that causes you anger. Then **scream.**

Yes, express your rage. Give your frustration a voice as you yell loudly. You can yell out a noise or a word or a series of words. Don't overthink this. Simply give voice to your rage. Ask yourself: **Who am I angry at? What am I angry about?** Write down your answer(s). You should note that one issue may come to the surface, or you may have several things come to mind. Jot down the first problem(s) that your body reveals.

I am angry at ______________________________

____

I am angry because ______________________________

____

Use your answer(s) above to fill in the tapping phrases below. Tap out the issue(s) that arise following the three-step EFT tapping method (the Setup, the Sequence, and Repeat the Sequence). For a reminder of how to tap, see the EFT tapping sequence located at the end of this chapter.

"Even though I am angry at ______________________________

because ______________________________,
I deeply and completely love and accept myself."

"Even though I am angry at ______________________________

because ______________________________,
I deeply and completely love and accept myself."

"Even though I am angry at ______________________________

because ______________________________,
I deeply and completely love and accept myself."

Pump the Arms

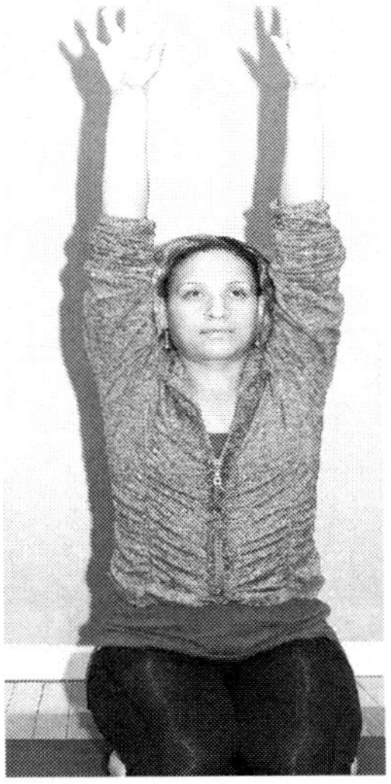

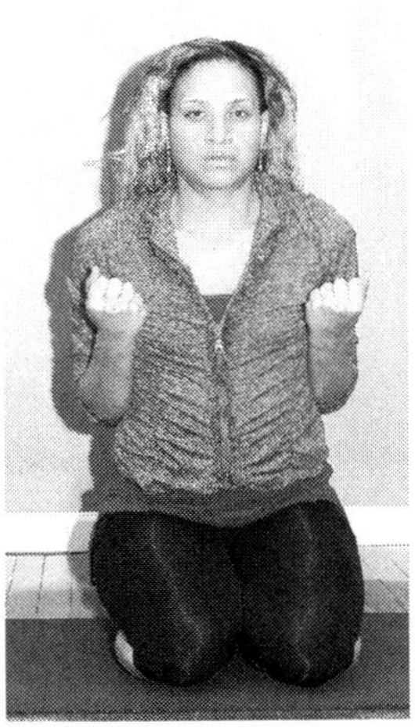

You can begin this pose either by sitting in Easy Pose or by sitting on your heels. Choose whichever posture feels the most comfortable for you. As you inhale, extend your arms towards the sky, spreading your fingers wide. As you exhale, pull your arms downward, bringing your arms by your sides with your elbows bent. On the inhalation, re-extend your arms overhead. Continue this breathing/movement cycle – inhaling and exhaling while reaching and pulling – as quickly as you can. As you gain momentum, pumping your arms furiously, connect with your internal feelings of rage. Perform this exercise for roughly 30 seconds to 1 minute as you focus on the anger that you feel towards yourself and the ways in which you punish yourself. Ask yourself: **Why am I angry at myself? What do I do when I am angry at myself?** Write down your answer(s). You should note that one issue may come to the surface, or you may have several things come to mind. Jot down the first problem(s) that your body reveals.

I am angry at myself because ______________________________

____

When I am angry at myself, I______________________________

____

Use your answer(s) above to fill in the tapping phrases below. Tap out the issue(s) that arise following the three-step EFT tapping method (the Setup, the Sequence, and Repeat the Sequence). For a reminder of how to tap, see the EFT tapping sequence located at the end of this chapter.

"Even though I am angry at myself because ______________________________,
I deeply and completely love and accept myself."

"Even though I am angry at myself because ____________________, I deeply and completely love and accept myself."

"Even though I am angry at myself because ____________________, I deeply and completely love and accept myself."

"Even though, when I am angry at myself, I ____________________, I deeply and completely love and accept myself."

"Even though, when I am angry at myself, I ____________________, I deeply and completely love and accept myself."

"Even though, when I am angry at myself, I ____________________, I deeply and completely love and accept myself."

FEAR/FALLING SERIES

Tree Pose (both sides)

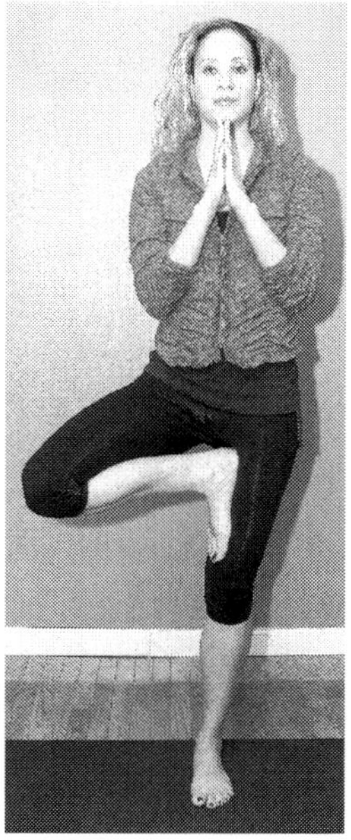

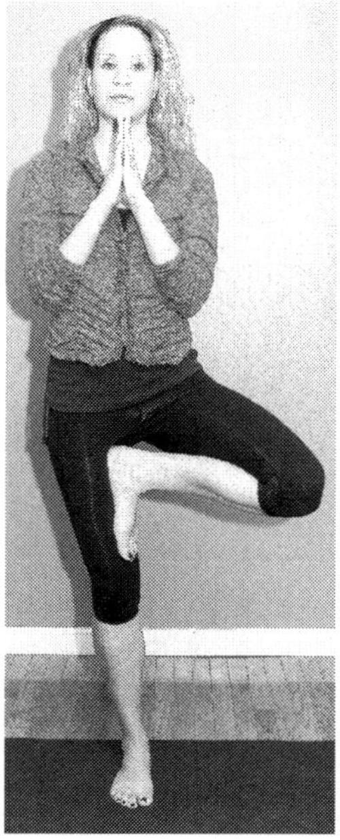

Stand on your yoga mat, finding your inner sense of balance. Shift your weight to your left leg, drawing your right foot up and placing the sole of the foot against the inner left thigh, calf, or ankle. (Note: Do not place your right foot against your left knee as this could potentially injure your knee). Feel the pressure of your foot against your leg and tune into your body's sense of balance, or lack thereof. Bring your palms to your heart center, pressing them together in prayer position. Because our physical fear of falling can act as a mirror for our emotional fear of failing, balancing poses can be a very effective tool for accessing fear. Tune in to the fears in your life that throw you out-of-balance and disturb your sense of equilibrium. Allow yourself to remain in Tree Pose until your balance is challenged and fear surges up from within. Come back to standing on your mat, shifting your weight to your right leg and drawing your left foot up along your right leg to take Tree Pose on the other side. As you balance in Tree Pose, you may find yourself swaying from side to side. Don't resist this feeling of precariousness. Your lack of physical balance will mirror other areas in your life where you don't feel grounded or stable. Allow your body to bring your awareness to your life's imbalances. Ask yourself: **What is the fear that takes me away from my internal equilibrium?** Write down your answer(s). You should note that one issue may come to the surface, or you may have several things come to mind. Jot down the first problem(s) that your body reveals.

I lose my inner balance because I am afraid of ______________________________

____

Use your answer(s) above to fill in the tapping phrases below. Tap out the issue(s) that arise following the three-step EFT tapping method (the Setup, the Sequence, and Repeat the Sequence). For a reminder of how to tap, see the EFT tapping sequence located at the end of this chapter.

"Even though I am unbalanced by my fear of ______________________________,
I deeply and completely love and accept myself."

"Even though I am unbalanced by my fear of ______________________________,
I deeply and completely love and accept myself."

"Even though I am unbalanced by my fear of ______________________________,
I deeply and completely love and accept myself."

Dancer's Pose (both sides)

Begin by standing in Mountain Pose. Shift your weight to your right foot as you bring your left heel toward your left buttock, bending your knee and taking hold of your left foot with your left hand. Lift your right arm toward the sky and spread your right fingers wide. Begin to press your left foot into your left hand as you hinge forward slightly at the waist, elongating your torso and straightening your right leg. Allow yourself to connect with the grace and beauty of this pose as you tune into your own expressive nature. Reflect back on your past, remembering the ways in which you used to love to express yourself. Recall the passions that you once wanted to pursue but have gotten away from or have avoided. Take Dancer's Pose on the other side as well while reflecting on where in your life you feel that you are lacking in self-expression. Ask yourself: **What part of myself am I afraid to express?** Write down your answer(s). You should note that one issue may come to the surface, or you may have several things come to mind. Jot down the first problem(s) that your body reveals.

I am afraid to express my ______________________________

____

Use your answer(s) above to fill in the tapping phrases below. Tap out the issue(s) that arise following the three-step EFT tapping method (the Setup, the Sequence, and Repeat the Sequence). For a reminder of how to tap, see the EFT tapping sequence located at the end of this chapter.

"Even though I am afraid to express my ____________________________________,
I deeply and completely love and accept myself."

"Even though I am afraid to express my ____________________________________,
I deeply and completely love and accept myself."

"Even though I am afraid to express my ____________________________________,
I deeply and completely love and accept myself."

Standing Split (both sides)

Begin in Standing Forward Fold, with your torso draped over your legs. Lower both of your hands to the floor. You may need to bend your knees in order to get your hands to reach the floor. Press your right foot firmly into the ground as you lift your left leg skyward. Internally rotate your left leg, equalizing your hips as you dip your nose towards your right knee. As you feel the downward pressing of your right leg and the simultaneous upward reaching of your left leg, connect with the experience of being split into two. Allow your body to forge a link between the feeling of being split into two and the difficulty that you feel when you are torn between two choices. Then, lower your left leg to meet your right and switch sides. Again, call your awareness to a situation in which you are troubled by indecision. Ask yourself: **What decision am I struggling to make?** Write down your answer(s). You should note that one issue may come to the surface, or you may have several things come to mind. Jot down the first problem(s) that your body reveals.

I am afraid to decide between ____________________ and ____________________

____

Use your answer(s) above to fill in the tapping phrases below. Tap out the issue(s) that arise following the three-step EFT tapping method (the Setup, the Sequence, and Repeat the Sequence). For a reminder of how to tap, see the EFT tapping sequence located at the end of this chapter.

"Even though I am afraid to decide between ____________________
and ____________________, I deeply and completely love and accept myself."

"Even though I am afraid to decide between ____________________
and ____________________, I deeply and completely love and accept myself."

"Even though I am afraid to decide between ____________________
and ____________________, I deeply and completely love and accept myself."

JOY SERIES

Breath of Joy

Stand in Mountain Pose. Make fists with your hands. As you inhale, swing your arms upward, reaching overhead. On the exhalation, bring your arms to shoulder-height, extending them parallel to the floor. Inhale, swinging your arms back overhead. Then, on your exhalation, let out a loud release breath (making a "haaa" sound) as you swing your arms toward the ground, letting your torso fold forward over your legs. Repeat this cycle of arm movements (up, side, up, down) and breath (in, out, in, "haaa") for several rounds. Move through these transitions quickly, but not so fast as to generate dizziness. Perform Breath of Joy for between 30 seconds and 1 minute. This pose will create an upward surge of energy as your body floods with adrenaline. Notice how the influx of sound and movement creates subtle, energetic sensations. While performing this pranayama, focus on where in your life you lack joy. Tune in to the areas in your life where you want to expand to the possibility of happiness, but feel unable to experience the exuberance that you would like to feel. Ask yourself: **Where in my life do I lack happiness? What is my biggest obstacle to feeling joy?** Write down your answer(s). You should note that one issue may come to the surface, or you may have several things come to mind. Jot down the first problem(s) that your body reveals.

I am unhappy with ____

____

The thing(s) that most get in the way of my ability to experience joy is/are ____________________

____

Use your answer(s) above to fill in the tapping phrases (below). Tap out the issue(s) that arise following the three-step EFT tapping method (the Setup, the Sequence, and Repeat the Sequence). For a reminder of how to tap, see the EFT tapping sequence located at the end of this chapter.

"Even though I am unhappy about ____,
I deeply I and completely love and accept myself."

"Even though I am unhappy about ____,
I deeply and completely love and accept myself."

"Even though I am unhappy about ____,
I deeply and completely love and accept myself."

"Even though ____
gets in the way of my ability to experience joy, I deeply and completely love and accept myself."

"Even though ______________________________
gets in the way of my ability to experience joy, I deeply and completely love and accept myself."

"Even though ______________________________
gets in the way of my ability to experience joy, I deeply and completely love and accept myself."

STRENGTH SERIES

Forearm Plank

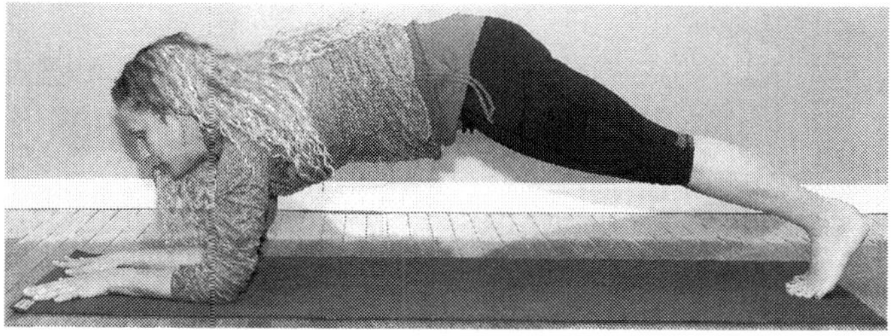

Lie down on your abdomen. Place your forearms about shoulder-width apart with your palms pressing downward into the floor. Curl your toes under as you lift your knees, hips, torso and thighs off of the ground. Your body should be parallel to the floor creating a flat, level torso. Try to hold this pose between 30 seconds and 1 minute. Feel the sensation of holding your forearms on the floor, activating your core, legs, and shoulders. Experience your physical and emotional strength. Feel the full extent of your body's fortitude, holding this pose beyond the point of comfort. Ask yourself: **Where in my life am I exhausted by having to exhibit strength?** Write down your answer(s). You should note that one issue may come to the surface, or you may have several things come to mind. Jot down the first problem(s) that your body reveals.

It is exhausting to be strong when ______________________________

____

Use your answer(s) above to fill in the tapping phrases below. Tap out the issue(s) that arise following the three-step EFT tapping method (the Setup, the Sequence, and Repeat the Sequence). For a reminder of how to tap, see the EFT tapping sequence located at the end of this chapter.

"Even though I am exhausted by my strength when I ______________________________,
I deeply and completely love and accept myself."

"Even though I am exhausted by my strength when I ______________________________,
I deeply and completely love and accept myself."

"Even though I am exhausted by my strength when I ______________________________,
I deeply and completely love and accept myself."

Upward Dog Pose

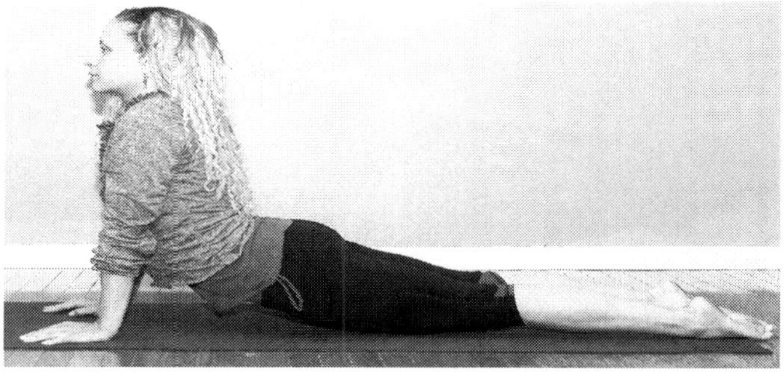

Lie down on your belly, stretching your legs behind you with your thighs touching and the tops of your feet on the floor. Bend your elbows, bringing your hands underneath your shoulders. Inhale as you press your palms firmly into the floor, elongating your arms. As you lift your torso off of the ground, keep your thighs firm, rotating them slightly inward as you narrow your hip points. After having held the strength-activating position of Forearm Plank and feeling the sensations in your shoulders, coming into Upward Dog Pose will open your heart and expand your chest. Notice how, after having to utilize your strength, you may feel restricted in your ability to open your heart. Feel your chest and shoulders expand after the stress and constriction that you experienced while having to be strong. Ask yourself: **Where do I want to let go of my need to be strong? Where in my life do I want to be more open?** Write down your answer(s). You should note that one issue may come to the surface, or you may have several things come to mind. Jot down the first problem(s) that your body reveals.

I want to let go of my need to be strong by ____

____

I want to be more open by ____

____

Use your answer(s) above to fill in the tapping phrases below. Tap out the issue(s) that arise following the three-step EFT tapping method (the Setup, the Sequence, and Repeat the Sequence). For a reminder of how to tap, see the EFT tapping sequence located at the end of this chapter.

"Even though I want to let go of my need to be strong by________________________________,
I deeply and completely love and accept myself."

"Even though I want to let go of my need to be strong by________________________________,
I deeply and completely love and accept myself."

"Even though I want to let go of my need to be strong by________________________________,
I deeply and completely love and accept myself."

"Even though I want to be more open by____,
I deeply and completely love and accept myself."

"Even though I want to be more open by____,
I deeply and completely love and accept myself."

"Even though I want to be more open by____,
I deeply and completely love and accept myself."

VULNERABILITY SERIES

Child's Pose

Kneel on your yoga mat, touching your big toes together beneath you. Bring your buttocks down upon your heels, separating your knees to a hip's width apart. Drape your torso over your thighs, relaxing it completely, allowing your spine's natural curvature to dictate the position of your arms, which can rest alongside your body or stretch out in front of you. Fully relax your body as you quiet your mind. Focus on the feelings of helplessness that you experienced as a child. Did being vulnerable bring you peace or pain? Was your youth innocent? Was it emotionally-charged? Go inward and connect with your inner child, reconnecting with the version of yourself that you used to be. Ask yourself: **When did I lose my innocence? What happened?** Write down your answer(s). You should note that one issue may come to the surface, or you may have several things come to mind. Jot down the first problem(s) that your body reveals.

I lost my innocence when I was ____

____

The event(s) that robbed me of my innocence was/were ___________________________

____

Use your answer(s) above to fill in the tapping phrases below. Tap out the issue(s) that arise following the three-step EFT tapping method (the Setup, the Sequence, and Repeat the Sequence). For a reminder of how to tap, see the EFT tapping sequence located at the end of this chapter.

"Even though I lost my innocence when I was ___________________________________

________ and ____

happened, I deeply and completely love and accept myself."

"Even though I lost my innocence when I was ___________________________________

_______ and ____

happened, I deeply and completely love and accept myself."

"Even though I lost my innocence when I was ___________________________________

_______ and ____

happened, I deeply and completely love and accept myself."

Cobbler's Pose

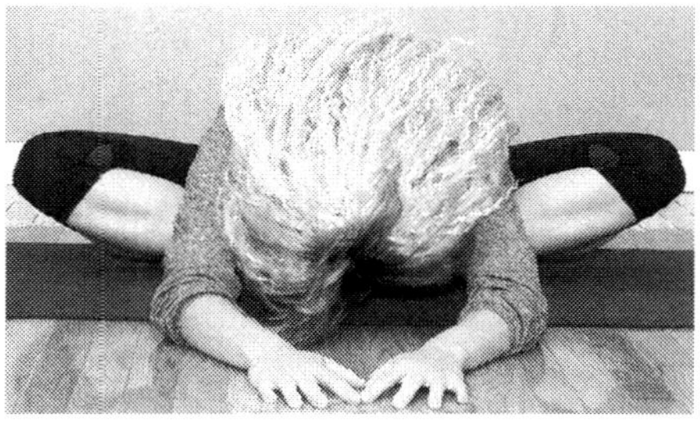

Sit on your yoga mat, touching the bottom of your feet to one another as your knees splay out to your sides. Keeping the outer edges of your feet on the floor, bring your heels in as close to your pelvis as you can. Imagine that the area contained within your pelvis, hips, and inner thighs is connected to your sexuality, creativity, self-expression, and self-actualization. Think of this central space, located within the diamond shape between your knees, as the container of your authentic soul. As you sit with your knees splayed open, focus on what it would feel like if you were to allow yourself to fully self-actualize and to live authentically. As your torso folds forward, covering your pelvis, connect with the ways in which you cover up, or conceal, your true self. Ask yourself: **What aspects of myself do I want to express that I don't allow myself to express? How do I cover up/conceal my true self?** Write down your answer(s). You should note that one issue may come to the surface, or you may have several things come to mind. Jot down the first problem(s) that your body reveals.

I want to express myself by ____

____

I cover up/conceal myself by ____

____

Use your answer(s) above to fill in the tapping phrases below. Tap out the issue(s) that arise following the three-step EFT tapping method (the Setup, the Sequence, and Repeat the Sequence). For a reminder of how to tap, see the EFT tapping sequence located at the end of this chapter.

"Even though I want to express myself by ______________________________,
and, instead, I conceal myself by______________________________,
I deeply and completely love and accept myself."

"Even though I want to express myself by______________________________,
and, instead, I conceal myself by ______________________________,
I deeply and completely love and accept myself."

"Even though I want to express myself by______________________________,
and, instead, I conceal myself by ______________________________,
I deeply and completely love and accept myself."

Reclined Cobbler's Pose

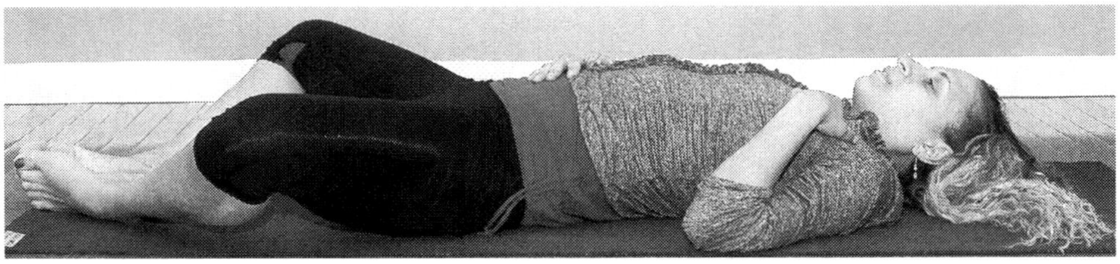

Lie on your back with your knees bent and your feet on the floor. Bring the bottoms of your feet together, allowing your knees to splay open, away from one another. Lay one hand on your heart and the other on you abdomen. As you press the bottoms of your feet together, settle your groin deep into your pelvis and allow your hips to spread open. Focus on a memory of a time when you truly expressed yourself – your wants, your needs, or your desires. Remember when you took the risk of being open and honest and were hurt in the process. Focus on the experience of being emotionally wounded. Recall the crushing impact of exposing yourself to the pain of not getting validated, of being rejected, of being ashamed. Ask yourself: **When did I risk being myself only to be hurt by someone else? Who hurt me?** Write down your answer(s). You should note that one issue may come to the surface, or you may have several things come to mind. Jot down the first problem(s) that your body reveals.

I took the risk of opening up and got hurt when I ______________________________

____

The person/people who hurt me when I risked being vulnerable was/were ____________________

____

Use your answer(s) above to fill in the tapping phrases below. Tap out the issue(s) that arise following the three-step EFT tapping method (the Setup, the Sequence, and Repeat the Sequence). For a reminder of how to tap, see the EFT tapping sequence located at the end of this chapter.

"Even though ______________________________

(persons/people) hurt me when I risked opening myself up by ______________________________, I deeply and completely love and accept myself."

"Even though ______________________________

(persons/people) hurt me when I risked opening myself up by ______________________________, I deeply and completely love and accept myself."

"Even though ______________________________

(persons/people) hurt me when I risked opening myself up by ______________________________, I deeply and completely love and accept myself."

LOVE SERIES

Sphinx Pose

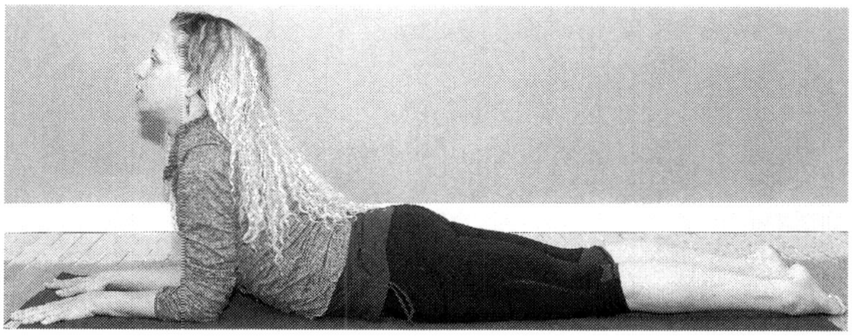

Lie face-down on your stomach. Squeeze your legs together, pressing your right and left thighs against each other. Lengthen through your spine as you rotate your thighs inward. Set your elbows underneath your torso and your forearms on the floor. Your arms should be parallel to each other. Lift your torso and head away from the floor, bending your back slightly. Keep your forearms pressing firmly against the floor to create more lift in your torso. Look skyward as you press downward through your forearms, hands and legs, and point your toes towards the wall behind you. Press your forearms actively into the floor, squeezing your shoulder blades backward, feeling your chest open as your back muscles contract. Press your pelvis downward. Feel your chest opening and the muscles encasing your heart spreading. Feel your shoulder blades pulling backward, toward one another. As your heart expands, allow yourself to connect with where in your life you lack love. This deficiency in affection may spring from your own inability to give or receive love or from the inadequacy of others to demonstrate their love for you. Ask yourself: **Where in my life do I lack love?** Write down your answer(s). You should note that one issue may come to the surface, or you may have several things come to mind. Jot down the first problem(s) that your body reveals.

I lack love ______________________________

____

Use your answer(s) above to fill in the tapping phrases below. Tap out the issue(s) that arise following the three-step EFT tapping method (the Setup, the Sequence, and Repeat the Sequence). For a reminder of how to tap, see the EFT tapping sequence located at the end of this chapter.

"Even though I lack love in my life______________________________, I deeply and completely love and accept myself."

"Even though I lack love in my life______________________________, I deeply and completely love and accept myself."

"Even though I lack love in my life____,
I deeply and completely love and accept myself."

Bow Pose

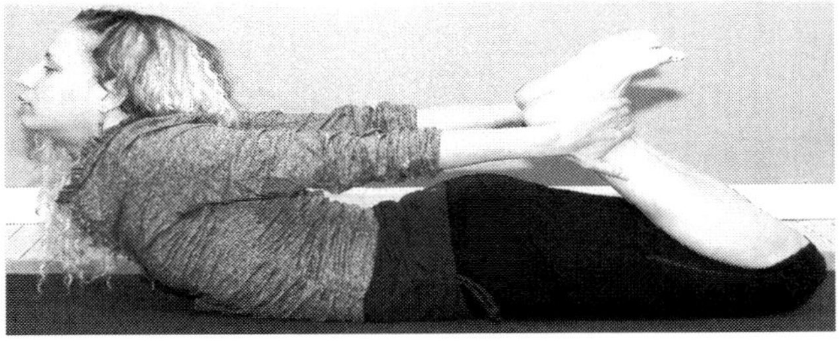

Lie on your abdomen with your arms resting alongside your torso. Bend your knees, bringing your heels close to your buttocks. Reach backward and take hold of your ankles. Keep your knees hip-width apart. As you inhale, lift your heels away from your buttocks and your thighs away from the floor. This will arch your back as you simultaneously pull your tailbone down towards the floor. In Bow Pose, focus upon the feeling of opening your heart, chest, and back. Imagine that, in pulling your feet back against your hands, you are unwrapping your physical heart. Feel as though you could tear open the gift of affection, as though love were a package that had been tied up like a present underneath the tree on Christmas morning. Untie your physical heart and unwrap the adoring innocence of your first love. Revitalize the early joy of that relationship. Reflect back upon your first love, on a specific memory of being enamored with someone else. Remember the ending of that relationship. Ask yourself: **Who was my first love? How did the relationship end?** Write down your answer(s). You should note that one issue may come to the surface, or you may have several things come to mind. Jot down the first problem(s) that your body reveals.

My first love was ____

____

The relationship ended when ____

____

Use your answer(s) above to fill in the tapping phrases below. Tap out the issue(s) that arise following the three-step EFT tapping method (the Setup, the Sequence, and Repeat the Sequence). For a reminder of how to tap, see the EFT tapping sequence located at the end of this chapter.

"Even though I loved ____
and our relationship ended when ____,
I deeply and completely love and accept myself."

"Even though I loved ____
and our relationship ended when ____,
I deeply and completely love and accept myself."

"Even though I loved ____
and our relationship ended when ____,
I deeply and completely love and accept myself."

INTEGRATION/DIGESTION SERIES

Half Lord of the Fishes (right side)

Sit on the floor with both of your legs extended in front of you. Cross your right leg over your left leg, with the sole of your right foot planted flat on the floor beside your left knee. Distribute your weight evenly between your hips as you take your left elbow to the outer edge of your right knee. Place your right hand on the floor behind you for leverage as you press your palm into the ground and look over your right shoulder. As you rotate your body in this seated twist, focus on whatever barriers might arise to keep you from integrating health and wholeness into your life. Identify all of the things that might get in the way of you incorporating the revelations and the awareness that you have achieved throughout your wellness journey. Ask yourself: **What gets in the way of my integrating/incorporating better self-care and healthy emotions into my life?** Write down your answer(s). You should note that one issue may come to the surface, or you may have several things come to mind. Jot down the first problem(s) that your body reveals.

The thing that gets in the way of my integrating healthier habits/thoughts/actions is ________________

____

Use your answer(s) above to fill in the tapping phrases below. Tap out the issue(s) that arise following the three-step EFT tapping method (the Setup, the Sequence, and Repeat the Sequence). For a reminder of how to tap, see the EFT tapping sequence located at the end of this chapter.

"Even though ____
gets in the way of my optimal physical, mental, and emotional health, I deeply and completely love and accept myself."

"Even though ____
gets in the way of my optimal physical, mental, and emotional health, I deeply and completely love and accept myself."

"Even though ____
gets in the way of my optimal physical, mental, and emotional health, I deeply and completely love and accept myself."

Half Lord of the Fishes (left side)

Sit on the floor with both of your legs extended in front of you. Cross your left leg over your right leg, with the sole of your left foot planted flat on the floor beside your right knee. Distribute your weight evenly between your hips as you take your right elbow to the outer edge of your left knee. Place your left hand on the floor behind you for leverage as you press your palm into the ground and look over your left shoulder. As you twist your body in this seated rotation, focus on whatever thoughts and feelings typically get in the way of your digesting self-love and accepting positive affirmations about yourself. Ask yourself: **What thought gets in the way of my self-acceptance? What feeling gets in the way of my self-love?** Write down your answer(s). You should note that one issue may come to the surface, or you may have several things come to mind. Jot down the first problem(s) that your body reveals.

The thought that keeps me from accepting myself is ______________________________

____

The feeling that keeps me from loving myself is ______________________________

____

Use your answer(s) above to fill in the tapping phrases below. Tap out the issue(s) that arise following the three-step EFT tapping method (the Setup, the Sequence, and Repeat the Sequence). For a reminder of how to tap, see the EFT tapping sequence located at the end of this chapter.

"Even though I don't accept myself because I think ______________________________,
I deeply and completely love and accept myself."

"Even though I don't accept myself because I think ______________________________,
I deeply and completely love and accept myself."

"Even though I don't accept myself because I think ______________________________,
I deeply and completely love and accept myself."

"Even though I don't love myself because I feel ______________________________,
I deeply and completely love and accept myself."

"Even though I don't love myself because I feel ______________________________,
I deeply and completely love and accept myself."

"Even though I don't love myself because I feel ______________________________,
I deeply and completely love and accept myself."

Supine Twist (both sides)

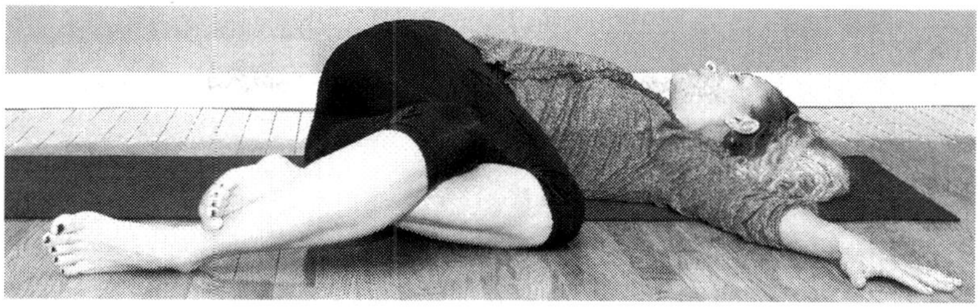

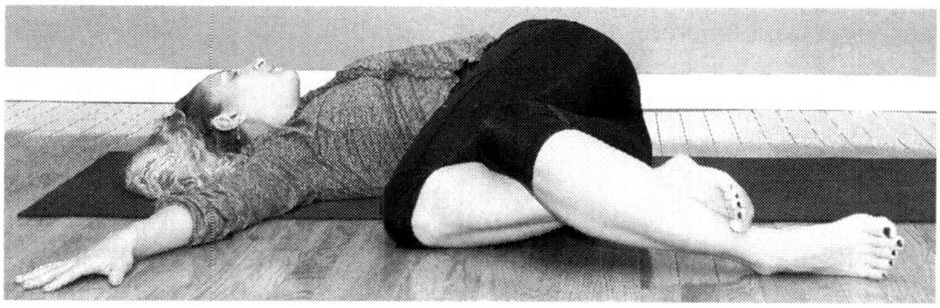

Lie on your back on your yoga mat, with your knees bent. Cross your right knee over your left knee and extend your arms out from your shoulders in the shape of the letter "T." Next, lower your knees to your left side and turn your head to look toward your right shoulder. Allow the twisting of your torso to churn up your feelings as the opposing rotation of the lower and upper body takes you deeper into the pose and the sensations. Take this twist on the opposite side, crossing your left knee over right and sinking the knees to your right side as you allow your body to bring you deeper into emotional awareness. Sometimes, we can feel as if we have been wrung out by our experiences, as if our insides have been twisted. Emotionally convoluted, we feel entirely out of sorts. Think about a situation or an incident from your past which you perceived as being "twisted" and which left you feeling as wrung-out as a sponge. Ask yourself: **What in my past was twisted/ warped and left me feeling wrung out?** Write down your answer(s). You should note that one issue may come to the surface, or you may have several things come to mind. Jot down the first problem(s) that your body reveals.

It was twisted when ____

____

Use your answer(s) above to fill in the tapping phrases below. Tap out the issue(s) that arise following the three-step EFT tapping method (the Setup, the Sequence, and Repeat the Sequence). For a reminder of how to tap, see the EFT tapping sequence located at the end of this chapter.

"Even though it was twisted that ______________________________________,
I deeply and completely love and accept myself."

"Even though it was twisted that ______________________________________,
I deeply and completely love and accept myself."

"Even though it was twisted that ______________________________________,
I deeply and completely love and accept myself."

ENDING SERIES

Corpse Pose

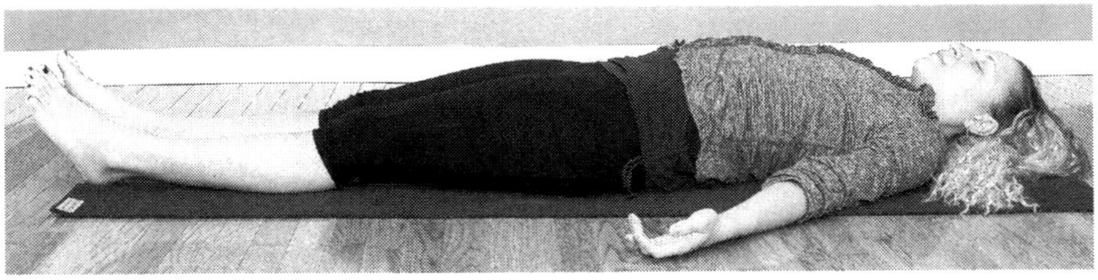

Corpse Pose can be a very powerful, emotionally evocative pose for many of people. The thought of lying still in this preparatory pose for our final rest (death), conjures up a plethora of emotions. Regardless of age, most people do not feel ready to let go of life. Lying in Corpse Pose brings up fear of the future, fear of death, anxiety about endings, worry about beginnings, spiritual crises, and internal turmoil. In short, lying down and allowing your body to let go may unleash a torrent of negative emotions within you. Lie on your back, letting your shoulders release on the mat, allowing your legs to fully and completely relax. Find a neutral spine. Think about letting go, your body like a corpse, entirely still. This may bring up some intense feelings in you. Breathe into them. As you lay in the posture of the dead, tune in to your emotions. Ask yourself: **What parts of me feel like they have died? What emotion/emotions do I feel when I think about my own death? Who did I love who has passed away?** Write down your answer(s). You should note that one issue may come to the surface, or you may have several things come to mind. Jot down the first problem(s) that your body reveals.

The parts of me that have died are ____

____

When I think about dying, I feel ____

The person/people that I loved who has/have died is/are ____________________________

____

Use your answer(s) above to fill in the tapping phrases below. Tap out the issue(s) that arise following the three-step EFT tapping method (the Setup, the Sequence, and Repeat the Sequence). For a reminder of how to tap, see the EFT tapping sequence located below.

"Even though ____
used to be a part of me and it died, I deeply and completely love and accept myself."

"Even though ____
used to be a part of me and it died, I deeply and completely love and accept myself."

"Even though ____
used to be a part of me and it died, I deeply and completely love and accept myself."

"Even though, when I think about dying, I feel ______________________________,
I deeply and completely love and accept myself."

"Even though, when I think about dying, I feel ______________________________,
I deeply and completely love and accept myself."

"Even though,when I think about dying, I feel ______________________________,

I deeply and completely love and accept myself."

"Even though I loved ______________________________
and he/she died, I deeply and completely love and accept myself."

"Even though I loved ______________________________
and he/she died, I deeply and completely love and accept myself."

"Even though I loved ______________________________
and he/she died, I deeply and completely love and accept myself."

The Setup… Repeat the setup statement three times while continuously tapping the Karate Chop Point:

"Even though I have this problem with (state the issue), I deeply and completely love and accept myself."

Karate Chop Point

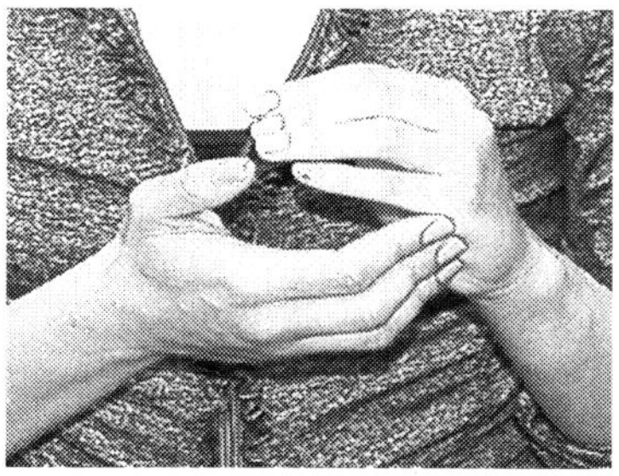

The Sequence… Tap continuously on each of the following energy points while repeating the Reminder Phrase (the issue) at each point. Tap as long as it takes you to repeat the phrase once, then move to the next point.

H, EB, SE, UE, UN, CH, CB, UA

H- Crown of Head

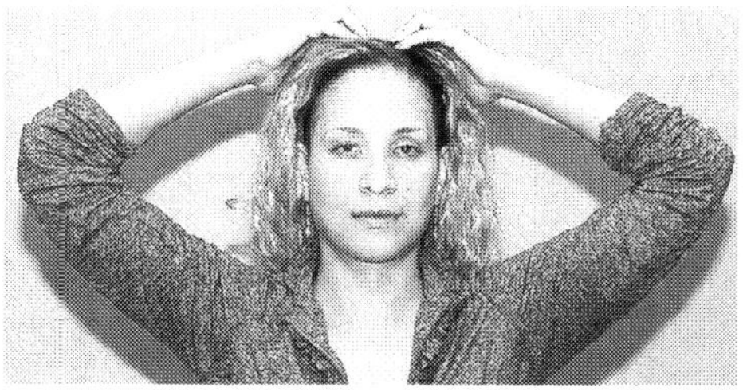

EB-Eyebrow

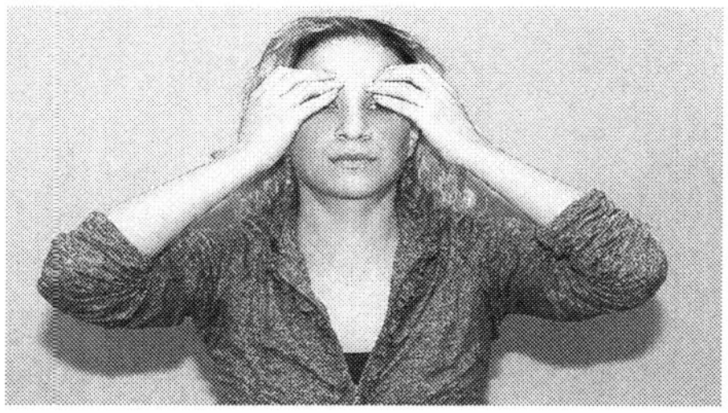

SE- Side of Eye

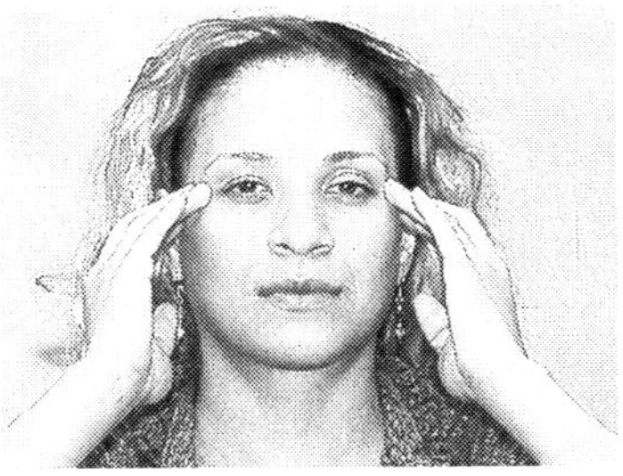

UE- Under Eye

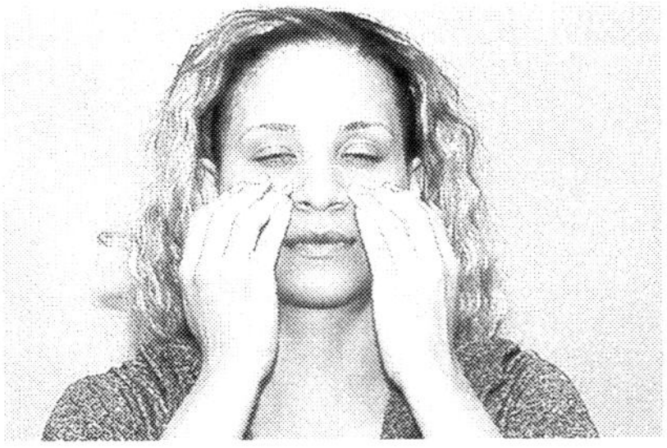

UN- Under Nose

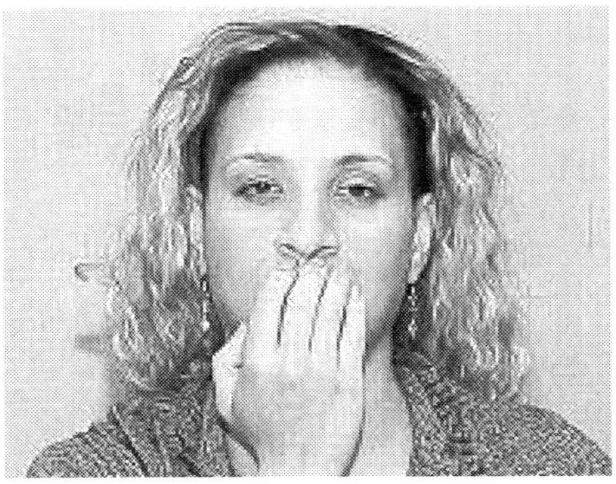

CH- Under Chin

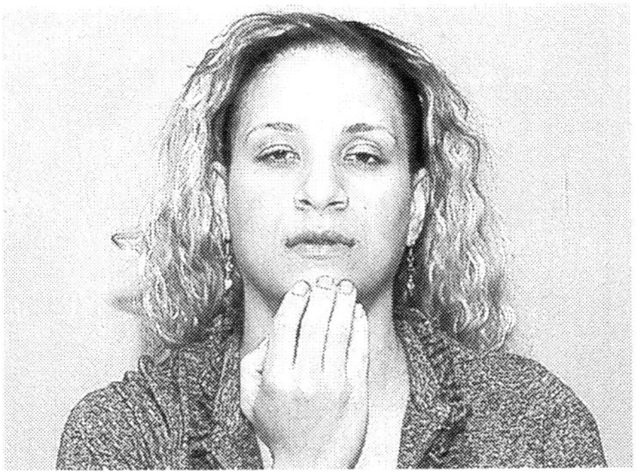

CB- Collar Bone

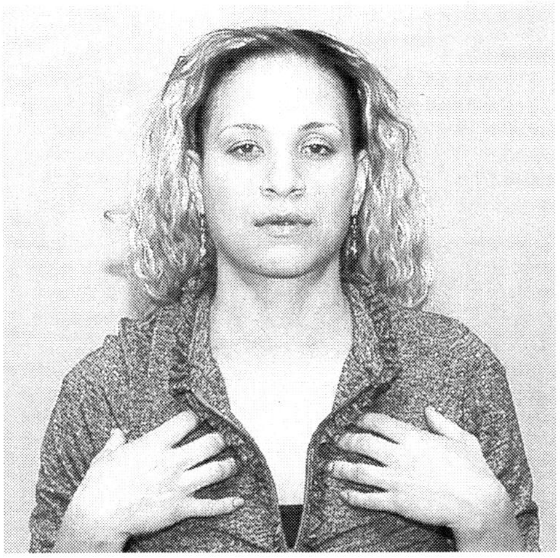

UA- Under Arm

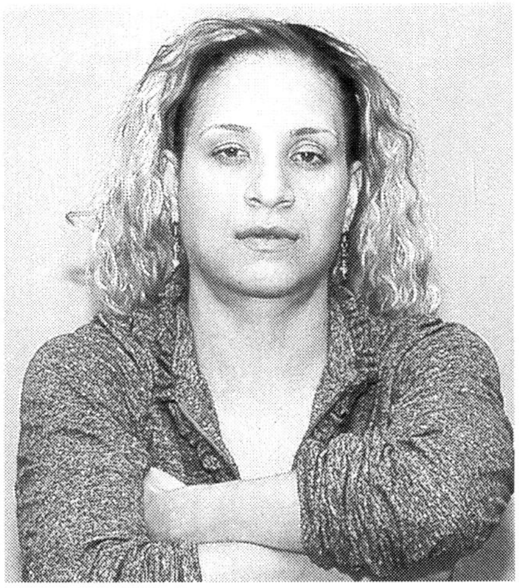

Repeat The Sequence... Tap continuously on each of the above-given energy points while repeating the Reminder Phrase (the issue) at each point. Tap as long as it takes you to repeat the phrase once, then move to the next point.

MORE POSES AND QUESTIONS

Now that you have completed your first EYE session, you might want to try some different poses and answer a few additional questions. The following questions are designed to elicit your deeply suppressed emotions. However, remember that these questions are to be asked of your body, not your mind. Trust that motion will lead to emotion. Ask these types of questions of your body while engaging in the corresponding yoga postures. Allow your body to respond to the questions and attempt to answer from a place of emotional and physical openness without analyzing whether or not your answers make intellectual sense. These pages are meant to be an additional resource, and I urge you to experiment with the following poses and questions and to feel free to make up your own. As you use your intuition, you will find that your body, and not your mind, has the power to liberate you from your pain. Awareness will come or it won't; however, healing will happen.

Yoga Pose:	Ask Your Body:	EYE Setup:
Standing Salute (page 119)	What do you want that seems beyond your reach?	"Even though I want (insert your answer) and I don't have it, I deeply and completely love and accept myself."

Standing Salute

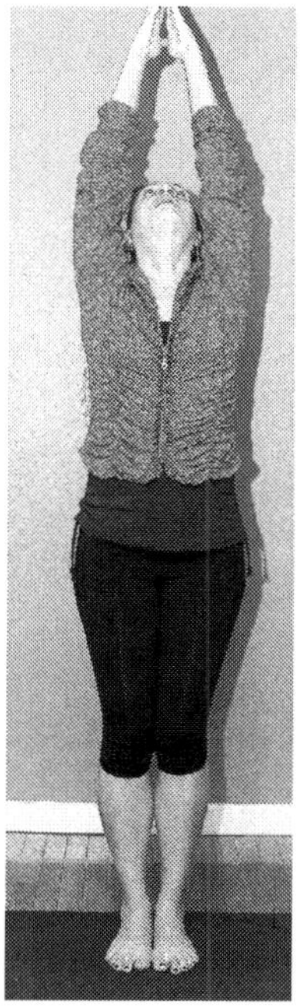

Yoga Pose:	Ask Your Body:	EYE Setup:
Child's Pose (pages 6 and 94-95)	As a child, what did you need/want that you didn't get? What childhood memory still troubles you?	"Even though, as a child, I wanted/ needed (insert your answer), and I never got it, I deeply and completely love and accept myself." "Even though, when I was a child, (insert your answer), I deeply and completely love and accept myself."

Child's Pose

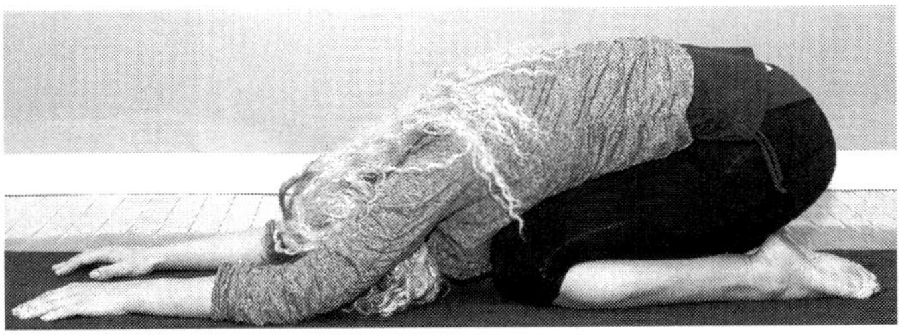

Yoga Pose:	Ask Your Body:	EYE Setup:
Bridge Pose (page 28)	Where in your life do you feel you lack connection?	"Even though I feel disconnected when I (insert your answer), I deeply and completely love and accept my-self."

Bridge Pose

Yoga Pose:	Ask Your Body:	EYE Setup:
Happy Baby Pose (page 9)	What in your life makes you feel vulnerable or exposed?	"Even though I feel exposed because (insert your answer), I deeply and completely love and accept myself."

Happy Baby Pose

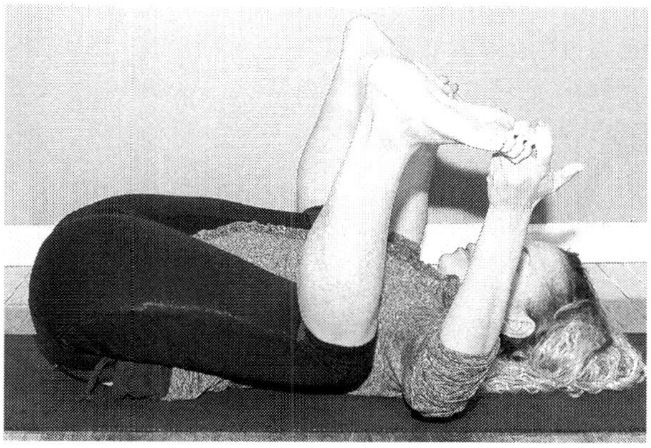

Yoga Pose:	Ask Your Body:	EYE Setup:
Gate Pose (page 118)	How old were you when you felt left out of a group/activity? What was the group/activity?	"Even though, when I was (insert your first answer), I was left out of (insert your second answer), I deeply and completely love and accept myself."

Gate Pose

Yoga Pose:	Ask Your Body:	EYE Setup:
Corpse Pose (pages 11 and 102)	What do you crave out of life that you aren't getting?	"Even though I desperately want (insert your answer) and I'm not getting it, I deeply and completely love and accept myself."

Corpse Pose

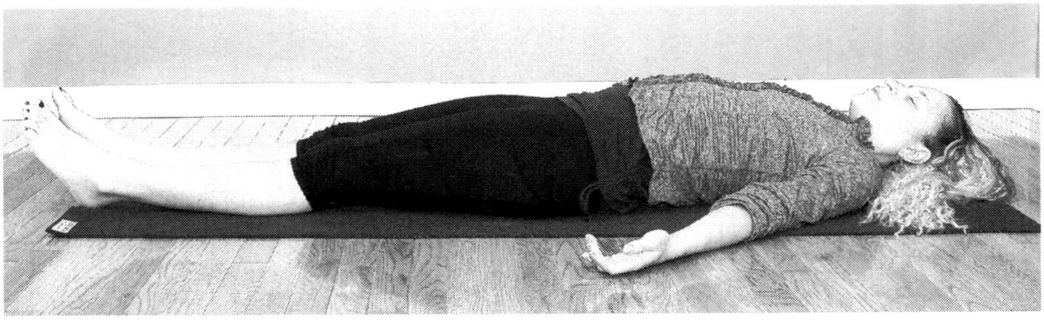

Yoga Pose:	Ask Your Body:	EYE Setup:
Modified Pigeon Pose (right side) (page 84)	What old feelings of shame are still holding you back?	"Even though I am still ashamed of (insert your answer), I deeply and completely love and accept myself."
Modified Pigeon Pose (left side) (page 84)	What old feelings of guilt are still impacting you?	"Even though I still feel guilty about (insert your answer), I deeply and completely love and accept myself."

Modified Pigeon Pose (both sides)

Yoga Pose:	Ask Your Body:	EYE Setup:
Easy Pose (pages 27 & 79)	What past memory causes you the most uneasiness in your life today?	"Even though I feel uneasy when I think about (insert your answer), I deeply and completely love and accept myself."

Easy Pose

Yoga Pose:	Ask Your Body:	EYE Setup:
Warrior I Pose (both sides) (page 14)	What self-destructive coping mechanism do you use to protect yourself from getting hurt?	"Even though I hurt myself by (insert your answer), I can protect myself without (insert your answer), and I deeply and completely love and accept myself."

Warrior I Pose (both sides)

Yoga Pose:	Ask Your Body:	EYE Setup:
Lion's Breath (page 16)	What is something you once said that you wish you hadn't said?	"Even though I wish I hadn't said (insert your answer), I deeply and completely love and accept myself."

Lion's Breath

Yoga Pose:	Ask Your Body:	EYE Setup:
Tree Pose (both sides) (pages 23 & 89)	Where in your life do you feel out-of-balance?	"Even though I feel out-of-balance in (insert your answer), I deeply and completely love and accept myself."

Tree Pose (both sides)

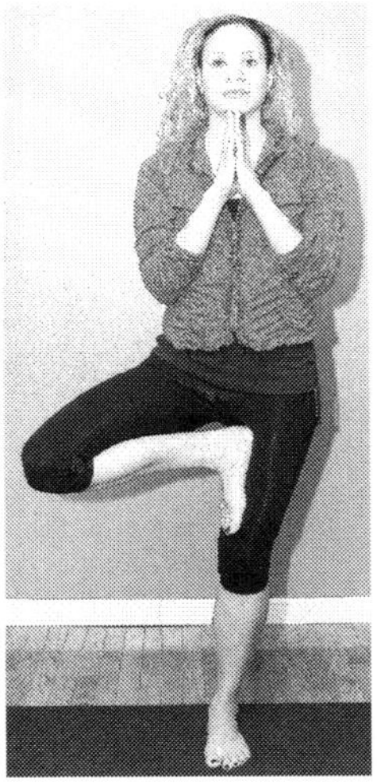

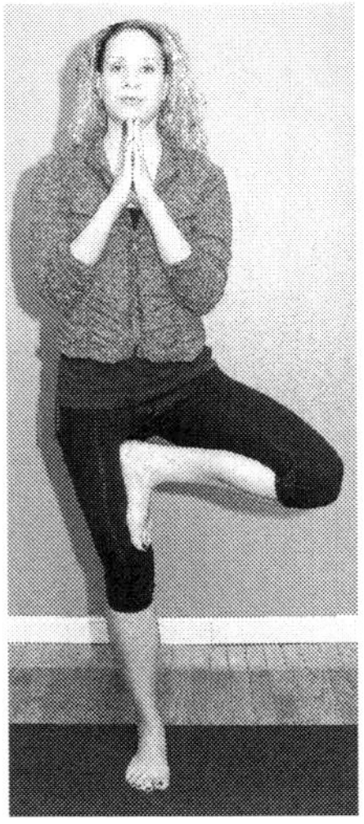

Yoga Pose:	Ask Your Body:	EYE Setup:
Neck Rolls (page 118)	What in your life (past or present) is it hard for you to look at/face?	"Even though it is hard for me to face (insert your answer), I deeply and completely love and accept myself."

Neck Rolls

Yoga Pose:	Ask Your Body:	EYE Setup:
Rabbit Pose (page 119)	What negative thought continually fills your head?	"Even though I can't stop thinking about (insert your answer), I deeply and completely love and accept my-self."

Rabbit Pose

Yoga Pose:	Ask Your Body:	EYE Setup:
Cobbler's Pose (pages 22 & 95)	What are you afraid to admit? What negative coping mechanism do you use to cover up your feelings of vulnerability?	"Even though I am afraid to admit that (insert your answer), I deeply and completely love and accept myself." "Even though I use (insert your answer) to hide my vulnerability, I deeply and completely love and accept myself."

Cobbler's Pose

Yoga Pose:	Ask Your Body:	EYE Setup:
Fish Pose (page 118)	What do you want to say that you stop yourself from saying? Who do you want to say it to?	"Even though I don't tell (insert your second answer) that (insert your first answer), I deeply and completely love and accept myself."

Fish Pose

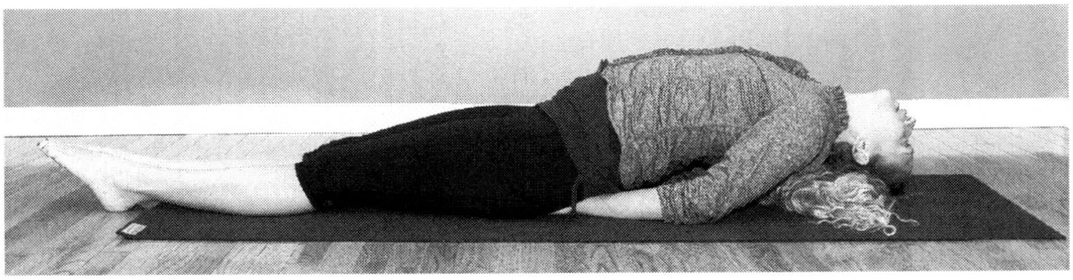

Yoga Pose:	Ask Your Body:	EYE Setup:
Mountain Pose (page 10)	What hurdle in your life feels impossible to surpass/ climb over?	"Even though it feels like it would be impossible for me to (insert your answer), I deeply and completely love and accept myself."

Mountain Pose

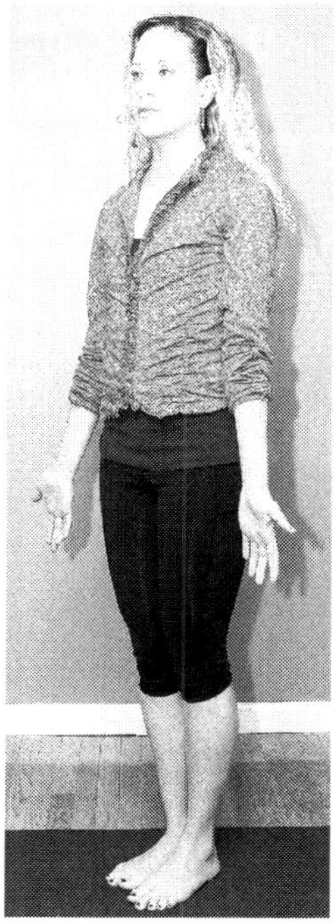

Yoga Pose:	Ask Your Body:	EYE Setup:
Sphinx Pose (pages 26 & 97)	Who violated your trust? What did they do that was untrustworthy?	"Even though (insert your first answer) violated my trust by (insert your second answer), I deeply and completely love and accept myself."

Sphinx Pose

Yoga Pose:	Ask Your Body:	EYE Setup:
Upward Dog Pose (page 93)	What has surprised you negatively?	"Even though I was surprised and shocked by (insert your answer), I deeply and completely love and accept myself."

Upward Dog Pose

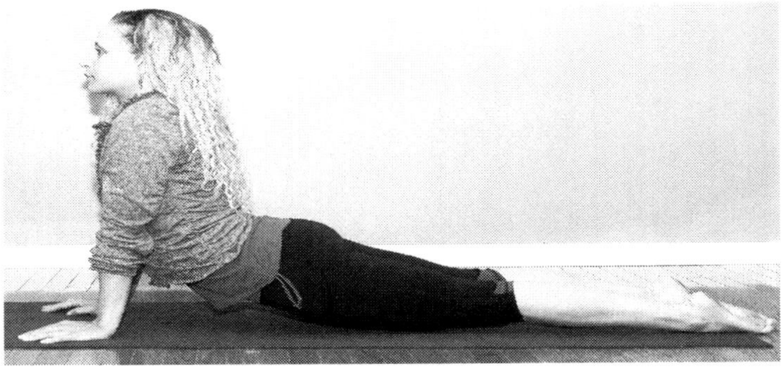

Yoga Pose:	Ask Your Body:	EYE Setup:
Camel Pose (page 119)	What in your life (past or present) makes you feel sad?	"Even though I am sad because of (insert your answer), I deeply and completely love and accept myself."

Camel Pose

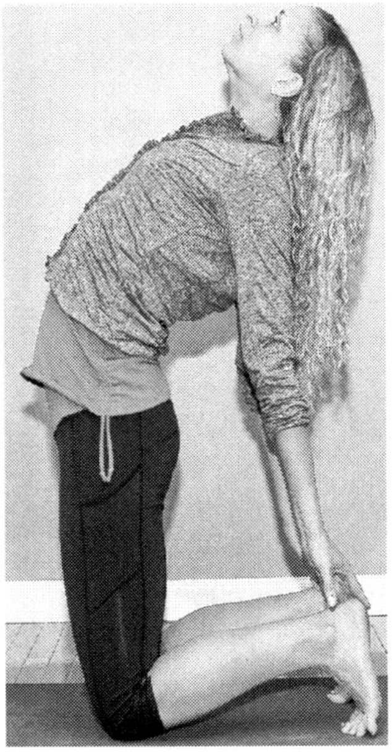

Yoga Pose:	Ask Your Body:	EYE Setup:
Frog Pose (page 118)	What is it that disgusts you about yourself or your life?	"Even though I am disgusted by (insert your answer), I deeply and completely love and accept myself."

Frog Pose

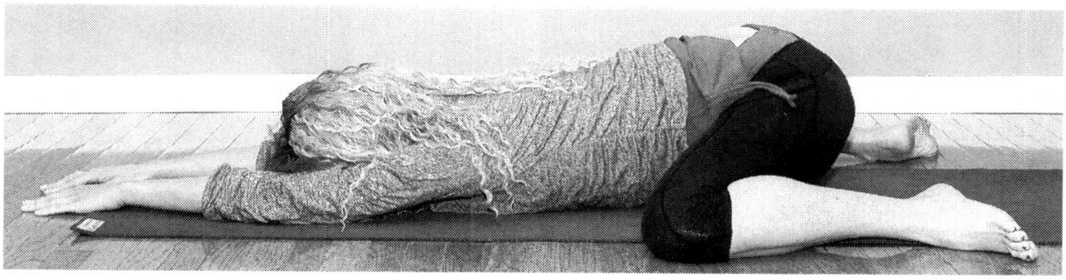

Yoga Pose:	Ask Your Body:	EYE Setup:
Breath of Fire (Optional Scream) (page 87)	What are you angry about?	"Even though I am angry about (insert your answer), I deeply and completely love and accept myself."

Breath of Fire

Yoga Pose:	Ask Your Body:	EYE Setup:
Reclining Hero Pose (page 119)	What did you want to be or do that you weren't able to be or do?	"Even though I wanted to be/do (insert your answer), and I wasn't/didn't, I deeply and completely love and accept myself."

Reclining Hero Pose

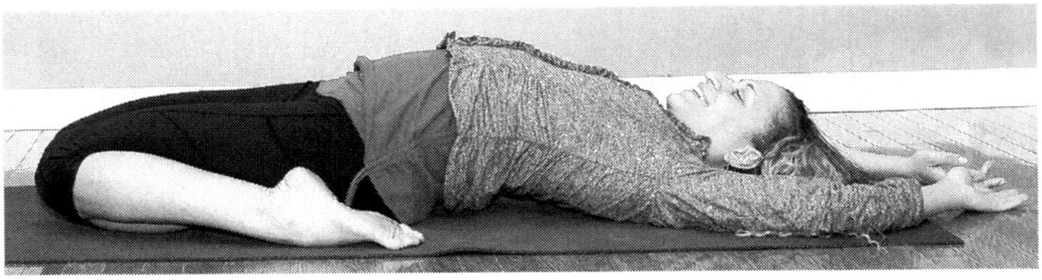

Yoga Pose:	Ask Your Body:	EYE Setup:
Prayer Palms (page 80)	What in your life are you pessimistic about?	"Even though I am pessimistic about (insert your answer), I deeply and completely love and accept myself."

Prayer Palms

Yoga Pose:	Ask Your Body:	EYE Setup:
Cat/Cow Poses (page 81)	Who in your life didn't love you in the way that you wanted to be loved?	"Even though (insert your answer) didn't love me the way that I wanted to be loved, I deeply and completely love and accept myself."

Cat Pose

Cow Pose

Yoga Pose:	Ask Your Body:	EYE Setup:
Wheel Pose (page 119)	What are you panicked about?	"Even though I panic when I think about (insert your answer), I deeply and completely love and accept myself."

Wheel Pose

Additional Pose Instructions

Camel Pose: Begin by kneeling upright with your knees hip-width apart. Rotate your thighs inward and press your shins and the tops of your feet into the floor. Do not squeeze your buttocks. Rest your hands on the back of your pelvis with your fingers pointing to the floor. Lengthen your tailbone down toward the floor and widen the back of your pelvis. Lean back with your chin slightly tucked toward your chest. Beginners can stay here, keeping their hands on their backs. If you are comfortable here, you can take the pose even deeper. Reach back and hold onto each heel. Your palms should rest on your heels with your fingers pointing toward your toes and your thumbs holding the outside of each foot. Keep your thighs perpendicular to the floor with your hips directly over your knees. If it is difficult to grasp your heels without feeling compression in your lower back, tuck your toes to elevate your heels. You can also rest your hands on yoga blocks placed to the outside of each foot. Lift up through your pelvis, keeping your lower spine long. Turn your arms outward without squeezing your shoulder blades. Keep your head in a neutral position, or allow it to drop back without straining or crunching your neck.

Fish Pose: Lie on your back with your legs and feet together. With your arms down by the sides of your body, make fists and bend your elbows. On an inhalation, press your elbows downward, letting that lift your chest high enough that you can place the very top of your head on the floor. Then, place your hands at your sides with your palms facing downward. Press your palms firmly into the ground and lift your elbows. This tucks your shoulder blades into your back and opens your chest. After several deep rounds of breath, place your elbows back on the floor, pressing them down. Lift your head, with your chin toward your chest, and move through each vertebrae of your spine as you roll back onto your back and slowly emerge from this gentle, neck-opening backbend.

Frog Pose: Begin in a Table Top position on your hands and knees. Make sure your hips are directly over your knees and your lower legs are parallel to each other. Lower down to your forearms and slowly separate your knees as far as they can go. From a side view, your hip joints will be in the same line as your knee joints. Your ankles will be directly behind your knees, and your toes will be facing out to the left and right, respectively. Your knees, hips and ankle joints will all be at 90 degree angles. Come to a depth where you can feel a significant stretch and still breathe comfortably. Try to relax your shoulders so they are away from your ears.

Gate Pose: Begin by standing on your knees. Stretch your right leg out to the right, with the heel of the foot on the floor and the toes stretching away from the body. Straighten your right leg as much as possible without hyper-extending your knee. Keep your knee facing the ceiling, your ankle in line with your right hip. Place the left knee directly below the left hip. Lift your left arm skyward, then slide your right arm down your out-stretched right leg. Your left arm will automatically begin to head towards your right side. Elongate your left arm. Each time you inhale, grow a little longer through the spine into the crown of your head, reaching into all of the fingers of the left hand. With each exhalation, gently deepen your side stretch, allowing the right hand to move further down the right leg toward the ankle and the left palm to stretch away from the left hip. Repeat this pose on the other side with your left leg outstretched.

Neck Rolls: Sit on your mat in Easy Pose. You may want to put a folded blanket or a yoga block underneath your buttocks for comfort. Cross your legs, slipping one foot in front of the other, and place your feet below your knees. Bend the knees and allow them to drop out to the sides. Begin to slowly circle your neck in one direction, holding in any areas of tension, breathing as you allow the tightness in your neck to dissipate. After several rounds of neck-circles in one direction, reverse the direction of your rotation, circling your head and neck the other way.

Rabbit Pose: Begin in Child's Pose, with your forehead resting on your mat and your hips on your heels. Interlace your fingers together behind your back. Begin to roll onto the crown (the top-most part) of your head as you lift your hips off of your heels. Roll the shoulders down the back, away from the ears, then lift your arms over your head. The top of your head will be on the mat in front of your knees. Breathe deeply, then reverse the clasp of your hands and stay here for several more breaths.

Reclining Hero Pose: Begin by kneeling on the floor. Your inner knees should be together and your thighs should be perpendicular to the floor. Open your feet slightly wider than your hips, keeping the tops of your feet flat on the floor and your big toes angled in toward each other. Press down evenly across the tops of both feet. Lean your torso forward slightly as you sit your hips back halfway. With your hands, reach back and draw the skin of your calf muscles toward your heels. Your back will round slightly as you do this. Sit down between your feet, resting your weight equally across both sit bones. Keep your heels and shins alongside your hips and upper thighs with your feet directly in line with your shins. Do not let your feet either splay wide open or turn inward. Allow your thighs to turn inward slightly. Press down on the tops of your thighs with your hands. Sit up straight and draw your should blades firmly against your back ribs. Broaden across your collarbones, drop your shoulders away from your ears, and lengthen your tailbone to the floor. Lay your hands on your thighs, palms down. Gaze downward toward your heels. Exhale and lower your back toward the floor. First lean onto your hands, then your forearms and elbows. Once you are on your elbows, place your hands on the back of the pelvis and release your lower back and upper buttocks by spreading the flesh down toward the tailbone. Then finish reclining, either onto the floor or a support.

Standing Salute: Begin by standing on your yoga mat with your feet about hip width apart. Root down through the inner edges of your feet as you raise both arms towards the sky, pressing your palms together. Look upward as you reach upward. Keep your abdominal muscles contracted as you extend your legs downward towards the earth and your arms upward towards the heavens.

Wheel Pose: Lie supine on the floor. Bend your knees and set your feet on the floor, heels as close to the sitting bones as possible. Bend your elbows and spread your palms on the floor beside your head, keeping your forearms relatively perpendicular to the floor, your fingers pointing toward your shoulders. Pressing your inner feet actively into the floor, exhale and push your tailbone up toward the pubis, firming (but not hardening) the buttocks, and lift the buttocks off the floor. Keep your thighs and inner feet parallel. Firmly press the inner hands and feet into the floor, tailbone and shoulder blades against your back, and with an exhalation, lift your torso off the floor and straighten your arms. Turn the upper thighs slightly inward and firm the outer thighs. Narrow the hip points and lengthen the tailbone toward the backs of the knees, lifting the pubis toward the navel. Turn the upper arms outward, but keep the weight on the bases of the index fingers. Spread the shoulder blades across the back and let your head hang, or lift it slightly to look down at the floor.

18804389R00072

Printed in Great Britain
by Amazon